INTRODUCING
Birds
TO YOUNG NATURALISTS

Number Nine: *The Louise Lindsey Merrick Texas Environment Series*

INTRODUCING
Birds
TO YOUNG NATURALISTS

FROM *Texas Parks & Wildlife* MAGAZINE

By Ilo Hiller

TEXAS A&M UNIVERSITY PRESS  COLLEGE STATION

Frontispiece: People are trying to make up for lost natural housing for birds by providing artificial nesting cavities, such as this bluebird's gourd home.

The paper used in this book meets the minimum requirements of the American National Standard for Permanence of Paper for Printed Library Materials, Z39.48-1984. Binding materials have been chosen for durability.

Library of Congress Cataloging-in-Publication Data
Hiller, Ilo, 1938–
    Introducing birds to young naturalists : from Texas parks & wildlife magazine / Ilo Hiller. — 1st ed.
        p.   cm. — (The Louise Lindsey Merrick Texas environment series ; no. 9)
    Includes index.
    ISBN 0-89096-412-2 (alk. paper). — ISBN 0-89096-410-6 (pbk.)
    1. Birds — United States.   2. Birds — Texas. I. Title.   II. Series.
QL682.H54   1989
598.2973 — dc19   89-4398
                                                            CIP

Come forth into the light of things.
Let Nature be your teacher.
—WILLIAM WORDSWORTH

CONTENTS

PREFACE

In 1855, when Indian Chief Seattle surrendered his land on which the city of Seattle is now located, he spoke about our relationship with the life around us. "What is man without the beasts?" he asked. "If all the beasts were gone, man would die from a great loneliness of spirit. For whatever befalls the earth befalls the sons of the earth. Man did not weave the web of life; he is merely a strand in it. Whatever he does to the web, he does to himself."

In these days when our technologies have given us the ability to manipulate our physical environment and its resources, including wildlife — for better or worse — the directions we take in the future will depend on what we have learned about the world around us and the "beasts" that share it.

Unfortunately, since the turn of the century, we have changed from a rural to an urban society, and a great many of our people have lost or are losing touch with nature and the animals that share our world. More than 11 million Texans (about 80 percent of the population) now live in an urban environment. Many of these city dwellers have forgotten the pleasures of spending time in the outdoors observing nature. They no longer take time to sit and watch a spider spin its web or wonder about the hummingbird's unique flying ability, which enables it to hover to sip nectar from a flower and then dart up, down, or backwards in an instant. Their children may even grow up without developing an appreciation for nature and a curiosity about wildlife. They no longer realize that they are a part of the "web of life." They are missing out on the fascinating world of wildlife that lies just beyond their doorstep.

My first book, *Young Naturalist,* was written to answer some of the questions children ask about nature by featuring general information about animals, plants, and earth sciences. This present book is the first in a series designed to introduce children to some of the interesting creatures that live within U.S. ranges — especially those we find within Texas — and whet their appetite to learn more about wildlife. No one is too young or too old to explore the fascinating world of nature. Like a giant classroom, it awaits those who take the time to enter and study what it is teaching.

Just as an iceberg shows only the tip of its structure above the water's surface, this book can feature only a few of the hundreds of species of birds that live within our borders. Those we have selected may or may not include all of your favorites, but we hope you will agree that each one is worth meeting. In addition to reading about their life cycles, you will also be able to take a closer look at birds in general and learn about their feathers, how eggs form, why birds sing, and how to set up a winter feeding station and build a bird house. I hope these glimpses will open a broader vista to you and be just the starting point for enriching your life with birds. You may find that you agree with aviator Charles Lindbergh, who wrote, "I realize that if I had to choose, I would rather have birds than airplanes."

Many of these birds features have appeared in the *Texas Parks & Wildlife* magazine during the past fifteen years. However, a few were prepared specifically for this book, and others have been rewritten or expanded. Special thanks are extended to Joan Pearsall, John L. Tveten, and various departmental biologists for research assistance. Recognition and thanks are also given to the staff and freelance photographers who have worked with me through the years to bring you these intimate views of nature.

INTRODUCING

Birds

TO YOUNG NATURALISTS

Introduction

If someone were to ask you to describe a bird, you probably would say it is a feathered creature that flies and lays eggs. These three characteristics do describe most birds, but the only characteristic that belongs exclusively to birds is the presence of feathers. Just as all mammals have hair, all birds have feathers.

It is true that all birds lay eggs, but so do many other creatures — reptiles, amphibians, insects, fish, and even a couple of mammals. All birds have wings, and most of them have light-weight bodies and strong wing muscles that make them well suited for flying. However, there are some birds that cannot fly, such as the ostrich and the penguin. Their wings serve different purposes. Penguins use their wings as flippers to help them swim under water, and the wings of ostriches help them keep their balance as they run. The presence of wings and the ability to fly are not exclusive to birds, either. They are shared by many insects, as well as the bat, which is a mammal.

A scientist would describe a bird as a warm-blooded (having a constant body temperature even when the temperature around it changes), bipedal (two-footed), air-breathing vertebrate (animal with a backbone), with fore-limbs modified into wings or winglike structures and a body covered with feathers.

Birds come in all sizes, shapes, and colors. They range from the tiny hummingbird to the giant ostrich. The smallest, the Cuban bee hummer, is only about 2-1/2 inches from bill tip to tail tip, and it would take about fourteen of them to weigh one ounce. The ostrich, which can weigh up to 340 pounds when full grown, stands about eight feet tall. Among the largest flying birds are the Andean and California condors, which have a wingspan of ten feet and weigh about 25 pounds, and the wandering albatross, which has an eleven-foot wingspan from wing tip to wing tip.

Different species of birds eat different kinds of food, and nature has provided them with different kinds of bills to make their food gathering easier. For example, the cardinal has a short, stout bill for cracking seeds. The hawk has a sharp, curved bill that is used to tear apart the animals it catches for food. The hummingbird's long slender bill helps it sip nectar from flowers.

Some people think modern-day birds can trace their ancestry back to the prehistoric pterodactyl (ter-ah-DAK-tel), but scientists agree that the pterodactyl was a flying reptile — not a bird at all. Its wings were similar to those of the bat, and it had no feathers. The true ancestor probably was a reptilelike bird called the *Archaeopteryx lithographica.* Its scientific name comes from the Greek words meaning "ancient wing" and "imprinted on stone." The fossil remains of the archaeopteryx (ar-key-OP-tah-ricks) were found in a limestone quarry in Bavaria about a hundred years ago.

A study of the fossil revealed that the reptilelike bird was about the size of a crow. It had a short, blunt, skinny bill and teeth, which it probably used to eat fruits and berries or possibly lizards and insects. It had the long bony tail of a reptile, but the tail was fringed with large feathers — a pair growing from each of its twenty-three tail vertebrae. Its feet and legs were very similar to those of the modern-day crow. Its feathered wings were small and weak-looking, and it did not have a breast bone large enough to support powerful flight muscles. For this reason, scientists believe it was a flutterer or glider. The front of each wing had three fingers, each armed with a claw.

These fingers probably helped the bird climb, pry into crevices for food, or grasp a branch to bring fruits or berries closer to its mouth.

It is estimated that this reptilelike bird lived about 130 million years ago during the time when dinosaurs roamed the earth. Evolutionary changes during the passing millions of years slowly changed this prehistoric creature into the bird we know today. As a probable carry-over from its reptilian ancestry, modern-day birds still have scales on their legs and feet, but they no longer have teeth.

In the following pages you will learn even more about birds.

Feathers

What a unique thing a feather is. It is one of the lightest and most flexible materials formed by any animal, and it is produced only by the bird. Although simple in form, it is amazingly complex in design, with all its branching parts.

To give you an idea of its complex nature, a six-inch flight feather from a pigeon may have as many as 1,200 feathery barbs extending from the sides of its center shaft. Even the shortest of these barbs may, in turn, have 275 pairs of barbules extending from its sides. To carry it even further, each of the more than 660,000 barbules has tiny, microscopic barbicels along it that end in interlocking hooklets. All of these tiny parts of the feather join together. If you separate them and then smooth them together, they will rejoin as neatly as a zipper closes.

Feathers are not all alike. They vary in size, color, shape, and structure. In fact, it takes several different kinds to make up the body covering of one bird, as the photograph of the different feathers found on a pheasant shows. Some, such as the wing and tail feathers, are smooth and relatively stiff; others, such as the downy feathers next to the skin, are soft and fluffy; still others are a combination of the two.

Each feather sprouts from a follicle, which is a tiny pit in the bird's skin. Blood carries oxygen and food to the growing feather through an opening at the base of its shaft, but when the feather is fully grown, this opening closes and the feather "dies." Since a full-grown feather is "dead," a bird feels no more pain when its feathers are cut than you feel when your hair is cut. If a feather is pulled out, another immediately begins to grow in its place. Feather growth is fast, often as much as a quarter-inch or more a day.

As the feather grows from the follicle, it is enclosed in a protective sheath of keratin (CARE-uh-tin), the same substance that forms your fingernails and the bird's beak and claws. These enclosed feathers give a baby bird a porcupine-quill look as they begin to sprout; however, once a certain stage of growth is reached, the tip of the sheath splits open and the end of the feather is released. With time, more and more of the sheath breaks away or is preened off by the bird until the whole feather is released and allowed to take its proper shape. Even though it looks as if the bird's entire body is covered with feathers, almost all birds grow feathers only from restricted, well-defined areas called tracts. The bare skin areas are covered by overlapping feathers.

At least once a year the bird grows a new covering of feathers. The follicles begin to produce new feathers that eventually push out the old ones. This process, known as the molt, enables the bird to replace all of those feathers damaged by the wear and tear of everyday living. Birds that have had their wing feathers clipped to prevent them from flying replace these cut feathers with flight-capable feathers during the molt and must be clipped again if they are to be kept flightless. The molt, which occurs just after the breeding season while the weather is still warm, also allows the colorful males to trade their bright breeding feathers for ones with more concealing colors. A second complete or partial molt the next spring will produce their colorful plumage again in time for the breeding season.

The molt is not a haphazard replacement of feathers, but proceeds in a very orderly way with only a few feathers involved at a time. Otherwise the bird would be both naked and flightless during the molt. Molting usually begins with the flight feathers and progresses in stages, so there are enough flight feathers at all times for the bird to fly. To keep the bird in balance, feathers located on opposite sides of the body are replaced at the same time. Once all the flight feathers are replaced, the body molt begins and progresses from tail to head. Waterfowl, however, molt in a different manner. They replace their body feathers first and then lose all their primary flight feathers at the same time. This leaves them unable to fly, and they must rely on the water and vegetation to protect and hide them from predators.

Other than flight, the main function of a bird's feathered covering is to protect the bird from the weather. However, to do this effectively, the feathers require constant attention. Birds must tirelessly preen—arranging, rearranging, smoothing, and waterproofing their plumage. An oil gland located above the base of the tail provides the waterproofing substance for most species. The bird transfers the oil to its beak by massaging the gland and then rubs its beak through the feathers to dress and waterproof them. As the bird draws the feathers through its beak, they are smoothed and arranged to its satisfaction.

Some birds, such as parrots, herons, and bitterns, have special feathers to provide a waterproofing dust for their preening efforts. These "powder down" feathers continue to grow as long as they are attached to the body; however, their tips disintegrate into a water-resistant, talclike powder. These special feathers may grow in solid patches on the breast or lower back, or they may be found throughout the plumage, as on parrots. Vigorous ruffling and preening distribute the powder over the bird's body and waterproof the feathers.

Feathers are a good insulating material. By fluffing its feathers, a bird traps many tiny pockets of air to hold in body heat and keep out the cold. The tiny air spaces formed within a waterfowl's feathers cause it to float high in the water as if it had a built-in air mattress. If these air pockets are destroyed, the bird's body floats almost submerged. When the insulating air pockets or protective waterproof qualities are destroyed by such things as an oil slick or detergents in the water, the bird's oil- or water-soaked feathers prevent it from swimming or flying, and it eventually dies from exposure to the cold water and weather.

When the weather is hot, the bird presses its feathers close to its body to eliminate the insulating air pockets so that body heat is allowed to escape. Since the molt also takes place during the hottest part of the year, fewer feathers are present then to insulate the body. The insulating quality of feathers is a drawback when the bird is trying to incubate its eggs. The feathers keep some of the body heat from reaching the eggs. To overcome this problem, the bird either sheds some of its breast feathers naturally or pulls them out to expose the bare skin. This bare area is called the brood patch, and egg temperatures next to it may be as much as six degrees higher than those next to the feathers.

Feathers also make birds one of the most colorful groups in the animal kingdom, but their colors can be deceiving. Most of the reds, yellows, oranges, and browns come from color pigments in their food and can change with their diet. If a yellow canary is fed red peppers, its feathers gradually will change to bright orange with successive molts. These pigmented colors result from chemical compounds called carotenoids (ker-AH-te-noids) that are depos-

ited in the growing feathers.

Blue, on the other hand, is produced by a colorless layer of cells with surfaces that scatter the light and reflect only blue wavelengths of light to the human eye. Greens are a combination of blue-reflecting structure and yellow pigments. Iridescent feathers have tiny ridges and platelets that reflect colors according to the angle of light. This explains how the throat of the ruby-throated hummingbird can flash from orange-red to crimson to black. It also explains the changing greens, purples, and bronzes of the grackle's breeding feathers.

When an excess of brown or dark pigment forms in the feathers, the bird will appear darker than the other members of its species. This condition is called melanism (MEL-uh-niz-um). If a molting bird is subjected to high humidity, darker colors may result. The complete absence of pigments produces white, and if this condition occurs throughout the bird's body, it is known as albinism (AL-buh-niz-um). Pure albinos are snow-white with red or pink eyes. The red or pink color in the eyes is caused by the blood showing through the unpigmented iris.

Feathers are so beautiful in color and pattern that people have used them for adornment for thousands of years. At times greed for these feathered decorations has endangered whole bird populations. Let us hope that we have learned a lesson from the past and will realize that a truly beautiful place for a feather to be is on the body of a wild bird.

Eggs

Located in almost the exact center of this unfertilized egg yolk is the white germ cell area. In a fertilized egg, this area is the point at which the young chick begins to develop. (The two brighter spots on the yolk are reflections of the lights used to photograph the egg.)

Eggs have become such a part of our breakfast menu that, except to decide whether to have them fried or scrambled, most of us don't give them a second thought. We eat them with our buttered toast and never even wonder how they developed. If someone asked you to describe an egg, you wouldn't have any problems because everyone knows that an egg is a small, shell-covered object that contains a yellow yolk and a substance called egg white. Although this general description is true, if you look more closely, you will discover that an egg is much more complex.

Perhaps the easiest way to study an egg is to go back to the beginning when it is just a cell inside the female bird and follow along on its step-by-step development. When a female bird is hatched, she already has inside her body the germ cells of more eggs than she will probably lay in her entire lifetime. At the age of three months, the young bird forms the first coating of yolk around one of these cells. As this

yolk begins to develop, another cell receives its first coating. This action, repeated in assembly-line fashion, ensures that there will be several yolks in various stages of development inside the female bird at all times.

Microscopic studies have shown that an egg yolk is made up of six rings, each with a white and a yellow layer. These layers are added to the cell in a strict rhythm determined by the position of the sun — the yellow layer during the day and up until midnight, and the white layer between midnight and sunup.

The springtime presence of a male bird causes a hormone change in the mature female, bringing about the creation of the final yolk layer. His courtship then triggers the finished yolk to break loose and fall into the oviduct, a tube that serves as a passageway for the egg as it moves through the next stages of development. Most wild birds cannot lay eggs if there is no mate, but this is not true of domestic chickens, ducks, and pigeons. Records show that

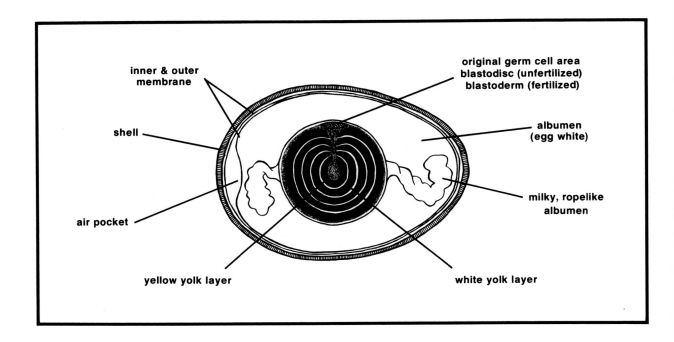

inner & outer
membrane

original germ cell area
blastodisc (unfertilized)
blastoderm (fertilized)

shell

albumen
(egg white)

milky, ropelike
albumen

air pocket

yellow yolk layer

white yolk layer

one leghorn hen laid 1,515 eggs over an eight-year period and never saw a rooster.

If successful mating takes place, the egg is fertilized as it travels down the funnel-like oviduct. Unsuccessful mating or the absence of a male, as in the chicken's case, produces an infertile egg, which will not develop into a young bird. It takes about twenty minutes for the yolk to travel down to that part of the oviduct where the albumen (al-BYOU-men) or egg white is produced. This albumen, like the yolk, is made up of several layers and is gathered by the yolk over a three-hour period. The first layer is but a thin covering; the second is dense and tough. It serves as a shock absorber to protect the cell during the egg's drop to the nest and during the shifting and turning of the eggs by the female throughout incubation. As the egg spirals down through the oviduct, a light, watery third layer of albumen is forced through the denser second layer and up against the yolk. The yolk now floats in this watery fluid, and the tiny cell comes to the yolk's surface.

If you have ever looked closely at an egg before it has been cooked, you may have seen the original germ cell. It looks like a small white speck on the yolk. You may also have noticed the milky ropelike matter attached to the yolk ends. These "ropes" are formed as the spiraling motion of the egg twists the albumen at either end of the yolk, and they keep the yolk anchored in the center of the egg. During incubation these ropes break, and the female bird must turn the eggs occasionally to keep the yolks centered.

When the egg has received all of its albumen layers, it moves on to be wrapped in two white sheets of tough membrane. Formation of these membranes takes about an hour and ten minutes. Then the egg drops into the shell-producing area of the oviduct.

One-fourth of all bird species lay white eggs; the shells of the rest, such as these bluebird eggs, are colored.

Here it stays for about nineteen hours while the shell is added in four porous layers. During the last of these hours, the shell receives its coloration. Although one-fourth of all bird species lay white eggs, the rest are colored in some manner. They may be spotted, blotched, or marbled with various colors, or they may be a solid color such as olive green or sky blue. The last eggs laid in the nest are often paler or have fewer spots than the first ones. Coloration also can vary from one bird to another within the same species. Since color pigments are obtained from the food eaten by the female, a difference in diet may be the reason for these shell color changes. Yolk color also depends upon the food eaten by the female. You may have noticed that your breakfast eggs sometimes vary from a pale yellow to a dark orangish yellow. Egg yolks of wild birds vary from very pale yellow to a dark red that is almost a maroon.

Once the egg is laid, air enters through the pores in the shell, and an air pocket is formed at the blunt end of the egg between the two membranes. This air cell provides oxygen for the developing bird during incubation.

Occasionally an abnormal egg is produced when something goes wrong with this natural assembly line. Double- or triple-yolked eggs occur when two or three yolks enter the oviduct at the same time and all are surrounded by the albumen, membranes, and shell of a single egg. Such eggs are considered rare. Records show that only one out of every five hundred thousand chicken eggs has two yolks and one out of every 25 million has three yolks. Yolkless eggs also may oc-cur if something prevents the yolk from entering the oviduct. In this rare case only the white gets enclosed in the shell and the egg is usually smaller. A chicken's yolkless egg will be about the size of a pigeon's normal egg.

If something goes wrong with the shell-secreting area or if the bird's diet has an extreme lack of calcium, a "soft-shelled" egg may be laid. This egg will be surrounded by only the two membranes. These abnormalities, although described for the domestic chicken, also occur among the eggs of other birds. However, considering the number of eggs produced, the errors are quite small.

Tomorrow morning as you eat your breakfast, stop and think about that egg on your plate and the miraculous assembly line from which it came.

Bird Songs

We all have our favorite singers, but none of them can match the skill of nature's feathered songsters—the birds. As you listen to their spring music, have you ever wondered how birds sing?

The human voice is produced in the larynx (LAR-inks), commonly called the voice box. It is located in the upper part of the trachea (TRAY-key-ah) or windpipe. Bird songs and calls, however, come from deep within the bird. They are produced in a tiny, two-pronged organ called the syrinx (SIR-inks) which, as a rule, lies in the chest at the lower end of the trachea and forks into the bronchial (BRON-key-al) tubes that lead to the bird's lungs. Although quite small, the syrinx is very efficient and can produce a song that is variously loud and clear or soft and muffled.

Sound occurs as air from the lungs passes over thin, delicate membranes within the syrinx. This passage of air causes them to vibrate, as our human vocal cords do. Special chest muscles change the tension of the membranes to produce the various sounds. In some bird species each bronchial tube produces its own music and operates individually. When both are used, the songbird actually is singing an internal duet with itself. Structure of the syrinx varies with the species and determines whether the bird's song comes out a whistle, croak, buzz, warble, or combination.

Melodious as bird songs seem to our ears, we can hear only a portion of the complex sounds some birds produce. Their songs may range from less than an octave to almost two full octaves, but the frequency or pitch of the notes many birds sing is too high for us to hear. Since bird notes seldom remain on the same pitch from moment to moment, slurring up, down, and in both directions, our ears often cannot separate even the notes that are in our hearing range. Up and down variations in the wood thrush's song may be as rapid as two hundred per second. With the help of electronic equipment, researchers now are able to record the wave lengths of these high-frequency, high-speed bird sounds and are learning more about them.

The top note a male tenor can attain is in a bird's low range, but a soprano's range of 250 to 900 cycles per second comes close to the 275- to 1,400-cycle range of the jay. A violin goes up to 3,000, and most songbirds can reach the 4,000 cycles of the piano. Wrens, starlings, and song sparrows reach high frequencies of 7,700 to 8,700 cycles per second, and other songsters can go even higher.

Although poets, romantics, and storytellers would have you believe birds sing just to spread joy throughout the land, the complex calls and songs actually are the birds' way of talking. Through the language of song the male bird proclaims the boundaries of his territory and sends out a warning to his rivals. From various points around his territory he announces that this bit of land is taken. If a male establishes his claim in an area where he is challenged by one or more rival males, he must sing more often to maintain ownership of his territory. Intruders usually can be driven away with a song instead of a fight. Bird songs are used to invite the attention of the opposite sex and help maintain the relationship between the female and male throughout courtship and rearing of the young.

Warning calls are used to alert the flock or family group of danger. A crow sentry sounds the alarm to the ground-feeding flock when all is not well, and the female duck quacks a warning for the young to hide when danger is near. Birds living or travel-

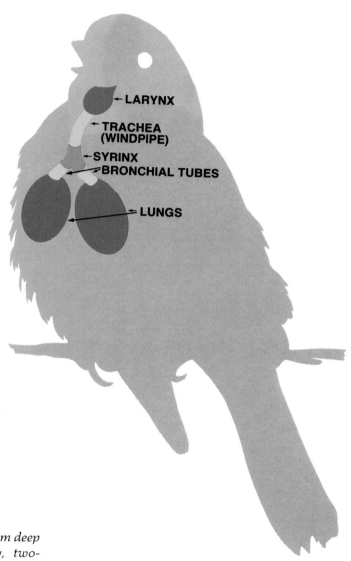

←LARYNX

←TRACHEA
(WINDPIPE)

←SYRINX
BRONCHIAL TUBES

←LUNGS

Bird calls and whistles come from deep within the bird, from a tiny, two-pronged organ called the syrinx.

Most birds, like this cardinal, have distinctive family songs.

Musical whistling fills the air as the meadowlark sings its territorial song.

ing together also have calls that are used to hold or gather the flock together. For example, when quail are scattered by the hunter or his dog, covey calls bring the group together again.

Most birds have a distinctive family song, consisting of a series of notes with a recognizable pattern and rhythm. The naturalist who learns these family songs can identify the species even when the bird is hidden from view.

Some calls are made by instinct, but research has revealed some interesting things about the adult song. At Cornell University some young bluebirds were raised in isolation so they could not hear the songs of any birds. During the first six months the isolated birds sang only call notes of distress and alarm, which researchers believe are inherited calls. At the end of the six months, recorded songs of the robin, oriole, and thrush were piped in, but the young bluebirds paid little attention to them. However, the reaction was amazing when the adult bluebird's song was played. The young birds cocked their heads, seemed to listen closely, and then attempted to repeat the sounds. Within five minutes all the

young were singing recognizable bluebird songs.

A few birds borrow songs from their neighbors. The best of these mimics, the mockingbird, has been known to imitate dozens of other birds. A mockingbird's medley may start with the oriole's song, but before it is through bits and pieces of the songs of the catbird, robin, thrush, and others may be tossed in. One report claims a mockingbird imitated fifty-five different birds in one hour of singing, quite an accomplishment.

Birds tend to sing most frequently during the breeding season. The air seems filled with song, especially in the early morning and late afternoon, which are peak singing periods for many species. Whippoorwills and owls prefer the night for their songs. If the day is dark and cloudy, they may start singing earlier in the evening and continue longer into the morning. Bird singing is governed by light rather than time of day. Weather also affects singing. Excessive morning coolness or midday heat may reduce singing, but mild temperatures increase the activity. Strong winds and heavy rain also stop or reduce singing, but periods of high humidity before and after a rain may

cause birds to sing vigorously.

Next time you hear a bird's song, enjoy its beautiful notes and be thankful we can hear even a portion of its musical language.

Bird Houses

Autumn is a particularly good time of year to try your hand at building a bird house. Even though a house you build in the fall will not be used by nesting birds until spring, getting it ready early will give it time to lose the odor of paint and newness. It may also serve as a shelter for a bird during the bad weather of winter.

You do not need to be an experienced carpenter to build a satisfactory bird house, but you should know that different types of birds require different size houses and entrance holes. The accompanying chart should help you to select the proper size for the type of bird you hope to attract. Detailed construction plans can be found in almost any book about bird houses, and a trip to the library should provide you with a variety. Select a simple design for your first effort, and when your woodworking skill grows you can attempt the more elaborate types.

Wood is, of course, the best building material and small pieces usually can be inexpensively acquired from the scrap barrels found at most lumber yards. In fact, many lumber companies do not charge for these miscellaneous scraps. Construction sites also are good locations to acquire small pieces of wood that are of no use to the contractor, but be sure to get permission before removing any wood from a construction site. Hollow limbs and sawmill scraps with the bark still attached make more natural houses, but this type of wood is not always easy to get.

The type of wood used is not of major importance, but cedar, cypress, and redwood probably will withstand the weathering process much better than the more commonly found fir and pine. Metal should be avoided as a construction material because it becomes quite hot when exposed to the sun and can actually roast its occupants. Since over-

Building and installing customized bird houses provides homes for cavity nesters, such as these bluebirds.

heating is so hazardous to eggs and young birds, even wooden houses should have ventilation holes drilled in the sides under the roof overhang to allow excess heat to escape. The roof should extend far enough to prevent rain from entering these holes and the entrance. Any water that may come in the entrance hole during a hard rain will drain out if small holes are drilled through the floor of the house at the corners.

Once the house has been built, you are faced with the question of whether to paint it or let it weather naturally. If you decide to paint, paint only the outside surfaces. Choose the more subdued colors, such as brown, gray, or dull green, for those houses being

SUGGESTED SPECIFICATIONS FOR BIRD HOUSES

Birds Using Single-Entrance Boxes

| | ENTRANCE | | DIMENSIONS | | LOCATION |
	Diameter (Inches)	Inches above floor	Bottom (Inches)	Sides (Inches)	Height (Feet)
Barn owl	6	4	10x18	15-18	12-18
Bewick wren	1	1-6	4x4	6-8	6-10
Bluebird	1-1/2	6	5x5	8	5-10
Carolina wren	1-1/8	1-6	4x4	6-8	6-10
Chickadee	1-1/8	6-8	4x4	8-10	6-15
Crested flycatcher	2	6-8	6x6	8-10	8-20
Downy woodpecker	1-1/4	6-8	4x4	8-10	6-20
Flicker	2-1/2	14-18	7x7	16-18	6-20
Hairy woodpecker	1-1/2	9-12	6x6	12-15	12-20
House wren	7/8	1-6	4x4	6-8	6-10
Nuthatch	1-1/4	6-8	4x4	8-10	12-20
Redheaded woodpecker	2	9-12	6x6	12-15	12-20
Screech owl	3	12	8x8	12-15	10-20
Sparrow hawk	3	9-12	8x8	12-15	10-30
Titmouse	1-1/4	6-8	4x4	8-10	6-15
Tree swallow	1-1/2	1-5	6x6	6	10-15

Birds Using Apartment or Colony Houses with Many Entrances

MARTIN: Entrance 2-1/2 inches, 1 inch above floor: rooms 6x6 inches and 6 inches deep; located 15-20 feet from ground. Should have at least 10 rooms and be placed in an open area.

Birds Requiring One or More Sides of House Open

BARN SWALLOW AND PHOEBE: Floor 6x6 inches, 6 inches deep; 5 feet from ground.
ROBIN: Floor 6x8 inches, 8 inches deep; 6-15 feet from ground.

Birds That Require a Platform with All Sides Open

SONG SPARROW AND BROWN THRASHER: 6x6 inches; 5 feet from ground.

mounted on trees or in the shade. Houses placed on poles in exposed areas, such as martin apartments, should be painted white to help reflect the heat of the sun.

Proper location of your bird house is just as important as its construction. Birds seem to prefer their homes firmly mounted on some type of solid support with the entrance facing south. The accompanying chart also will give you an idea how high the house should be mounted. Houses that are hung from a wire and allowed to twist and swing in the wind are seldom used. Martins, bluebirds, and flycatchers prefer to have their homes out in the open with no trees or buildings too near. Birds

also are very territorial and require a certain amount of space around their nesting area. As a result, houses placed too close to each other often cause conflicts, and the birds may abandon them altogether.

Cats and fox squirrels are always a threat to nesting birds and their young, so it may be necessary to add a predator shield to the post or tree on which you mount your bird house. Probably the most effective type of shield is a sheet-metal, cone-shaped device about eighteen inches long. Fasten this shield high enough on the tree or post to prevent the predator from jumping above it to gain a foothold.

After the bird house is mounted and

protected, you should not have to do anything else until the middle of March. At that time you should check the house to be sure it is free of mud daubers, bees, mice, and flying squirrels, which sometimes move into a vacant bird house. If you were wise and built your house with either a hinged or sliding roof, front or bottom, this cleaning chore will be quite simple.

When the birds are through nesting, the bird house should again be cleaned to get rid of any parasites, such as fleas, bird lice, and bird flies, which may have moved in with the first occupants. If you do this, the next resident will not be infested with the parasites left by the previous nester.

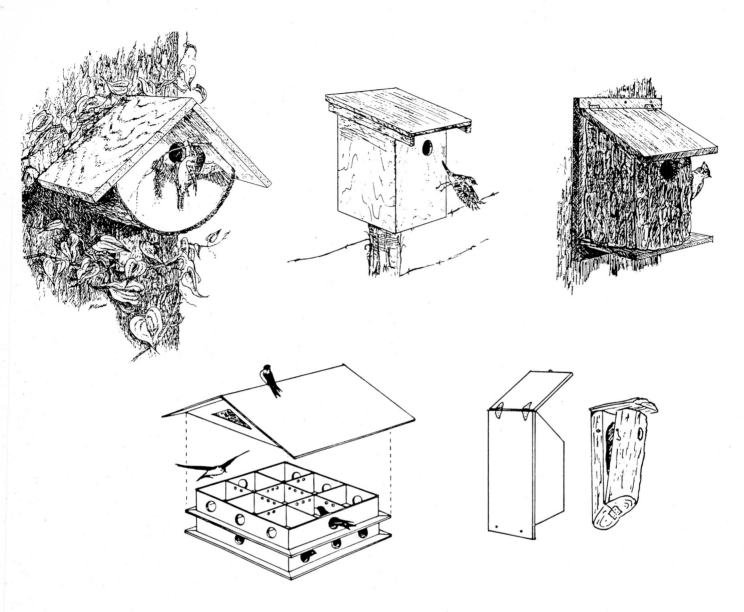

Do not put nesting materials inside your bird house to encourage its use. Most birds are very selective and prefer to gather each piece and arrange it to suit themselves. However, if you build a house meant for a woodpecker or owl, put about an inch of sawdust or wood shavings in the bottom for the eggs because these birds do not gather nesting materials. Detailed instructions for building a bluebird house are in the chapter on bluebirds.

Robins, thrashers, and phoebes do not nest in houses but sometimes will use man-made nesting platforms. The accompanying chart will give you the dimensions required by these birds in case you want to try your hand at building one of these nesting platforms.

When spring arrives and your bird houses or platforms are occupied by busy nesters that will provide beauty, hours of entertainment and nature study, and possible bug exterminating services, you will be glad you took the time to build the houses or platforms.

There are many kinds of birdhouses, ranging from simple to the more elaborate type, such as the purple martin apartment house, bottom left.

Bird Feeders

Many people place feeders in their yards in the spring to attract birds. They enjoy having the birds around and may spend hours sitting outside watching them. However, when winter arrives and it gets too cold to sit outdoors, such feeding programs may stop. Birds need a steady supply of food to generate the energy needed to keep their bodies warm in winter. Unfortunately, those attracted to the now-abandoned feeders discover their easy food supply is cut off just when natural foods are harder to find. If feeding programs are not going to be continued all year, the birds would be better off if the handouts were saved for the winter months.

To make life a little easier for the birds in your neighborhood this winter, you might consider setting up a feeding station. It will provide a supply of food for them until spring when natural foods such as seeds, berries, and insects are easier to find. Once you start a feeding program, try to continue it all winter. The birds you attract may be depending on your handouts.

A well-equipped winter feeding station should have a feeder of some type for seeds, a container for suet or birdseed cake mixtures, and a water source. Wild bird seed and commercial feeders can be purchased, but if you want to be more personally involved, you might build your own.

A square, gallon-sized plastic milk jug can be converted into a simple feeder quite easily. It may not be as attractive as a commercial feeder, but the birds won't mind. Cut openings about three inches wide and four inches high, in the two sides opposite the handle. They should be about two and a half inches from the bottom of the jug. Arching the tops of these openings will make them more decorative. (A hobby knife is a good tool for this job, but because these knives usually are very

Pie Pan Feeder

sharp, it would be wise for children to have adult help or supervision. In fact, most of the activities connected with building an outdoor feeding station may need some adult assistance.)

Add perches to the milk-jug feeder by drilling a set of holes through the jug about one-fourth inch below one of the openings. Insert a wooden dowel through these holes. Drill another set of holes through the jug one-half inch below the other opening and insert a second dowel. The ends should extend about two inches on the sides with the openings to form perches. Drilling one set of holes lower than the other set allows the dowels to cross inside the jug.

Attach the milk jug feeder to a piece of wood with a couple of wood screws through the handle. Mount the pieces of wood on a post, tree, or the house and your feeder is ready to use.

Milk Jug Feeder

Another simple feeder can be made out of a wide-mouth quart jar, an aluminum foil pie pan, a few scraps of wood or Masonite 3/4 inch wide, 1/4 inch thick, and 6-3/4 inches long. Divide the strip into three pieces — one 3-1/2 inches long and two 1-3/8 inches long. Attach them to the outside of the lid in the shape of a cross using short U-shaped nails. Drive them into the wood from the inside of the lid. Drill a 1/2-inch hole in each of the four spaces on the lid not covered by wood strips.

Place the lid, wood-strip side down, in the center of the pie pan. Set the pan on a 9-inch square or round piece of wood or Masonite. Drill a 1/4-inch hole through the center of the lid, pan, and wood. Put a bolt through the hole and attach a nut to the bottom to hold all the pieces together. Drill three evenly spaced holes through the wood to which the pan is attached. Insert the 30-inch pieces of rope or cord in the holes. Tie the ends of the cords together under the feeder and at the top. Fill the

jar with birdseed, screw on the lid assembly, and quickly turn the unit over. The seed will flow into the pan through the holes in the lid, and as the birds eat the available seed, more will flow out to replace it. Hang the feeder from a tree limb or post.

A platform feeder also is easy to make, but you have to clean it often to keep the food from becoming contaminated with bird droppings that might cause disease. To build it, just attach a raised edge to a two- or three-foot square piece of wood. This edging, which keeps the seeds from blowing off, should have an open space on one side so water can drain off. Adding a roof and placing glass or Plexiglass on three sides will protect the birds and food from wind and weather. Wooden sides also offer protection, but you can't watch the feeding birds through them. The platform feeder usually is attached to a post or windowsill, but it also can be hung from a tree limb.

The hopper-type feeder resembles a flip-up mailbox, except the front is glass or Plexiglass and slants inward at the bottom. A space between the bottom of the glass and the feeding tray allows the seeds to flow out as needed. The food is protected, the clear front lets you see how much food it contains, and the flip top makes it easy to fill. The hopper-type feeder can be attached to a tree, post, or house.

After you have made or bought a feeder, you must decide where to put it. The south side of the house offers protection from the cold north wind and the east side is exposed to the warming rays of the morning sun. Both locations are suitable. Cats and squirrels also must be taken into consideration when you are choosing a location for your feeder. Cats, of course, want to eat the birds, and squirrels want the birds' food. Be sure to hang the feeder

far enough off the ground to be out of jumping range, and check for nearby limbs that could serve as launching pads. A cone-shaped metal shield can be added to a post-mounted feeder to stop animals from climbing it.

The basic food for your feeder is a combination of seeds, and hungry birds can consume a lot of it. Even insect-eating birds eat seeds in winter when insects are not available. Commercial wild bird seed mixtures may include all or a few of the following ingredients: millet, milo, cracked corn, buckwheat, canary grass seed, sorghum, sunflower seeds, barley, hempseed, oats, safflower, and peanut hearts. These commercial mixtures are excellent, but they can be expensive over a long period.

More economical homemade seed mixtures may be prepared by buying a few basic ingredients in large quantities from feed stores or seed wholesalers. Sunflower seeds, hempseed, millet, buckwheat, and cracked corn combine to make a balanced homemade mixture. Rice, coarse oatmeal, dried bread crumbs, shelled nuts (not the roasted or salted type), and cereals can be added to your homemade mixture for variety. When birds feed naturally on the ground, they obtain a certain amount of grit that is needed to digest their food. If the mixture you use in your feeder does not contain grit, you will need to add to it. A teaspoon of fine sand, crushed eggshells, or crushed charcoal added to each quart of seed will meet the birds' digestive needs.

Although it won't fit in some of your seed feeders, fruit can be placed on a platform feeder for hungry birds. Small pieces of apples, oranges, bananas, tomatoes, and grapes are welcome handouts. Fruit that may be too ripe for most people to eat is just right for the birds. Check with the produce man at

Platform Feeder

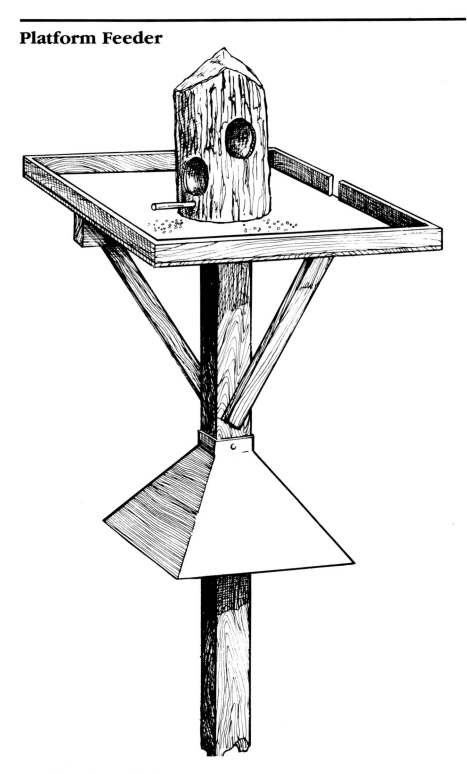

your local grocery store for special prices on overripe fruits.

Since birds need high-energy foods in winter, suet is another good thing to provide. Suet is the hard fat or tallow found around the kidneys and loins of beef and sheep. It can be purchased at the grocery store meat counter. Tie chunks of raw suet to a tree, or place it in small bags made from fiber-type onion sacks or netting. Attach these bags to trees or posts. Melted suet also can be used as a base for birdseed cakes. The recipes and serving containers for these mixtures can be as varied as your imagination.

Making a log feeder for suet seed-cake mixtures requires some wood-working skills, but the feeder will be an attractive addition to your feeding station. Drill a few quarter-sized holes about an inch deep in a small log. Leave the bark on it to provide footholds for clinging birds, and insert small dowels or sticks below a few of the holes to form perches for other bird species. Attach an eye bolt at one end, and the feeder is ready to hang from a nearby branch. Or, level off one end and attach the log to a platform feeder.

A foot-square, two-inch block of wood with a pattern of holes drilled an inch deep into its flat surface will make a tray-type seedcake feeder. It can be mounted on a post, set on the ground, or hung from a tree limb. To hang it, just drill holes in the corners (or use screw eyes) and attach cords.

If you don't have the materials or tools to make this tray-type feeder, an old muffin tin can be used as a substitute. And, if you look around the house, you probably will find quite a few things that can be used to hold the suet mixture. The shell from half a grapefruit or orange, foil pie pans, and plastic butter tubs are a few examples. Once you have decided on your con-

Seed Cake Feeder

Hopper-Type Feeder

tainer, the next step is to make the bird-seed cake mixture. With some assistance from an adult, grind or cut the suet into small pieces, place it in a double boiler and let it melt completely. Allow it to cool and harden. Melting it again will give it a firmer texture when it hardens the second time, and it will hold the ingredients better.

The ingredients can be a combination of almost anything animal or vegetable. Some suggested items are: dried ground meat, cooked and chopped bacon rind, millet, sunflower seeds, rice, oatmeal, dried bread crumbs, cereal, corn meal, cracked corn, raw nuts, and raisins. Stir the selected ingredients into the melted suet just before it hardens. Mold it in the containers you have gathered, stuff it in the holes of your

log or wood feeders, or spread it on the bark of a tree.

Peanut butter, although more expensive, is a high-energy food that can be used instead of suet in a birdseed cake mixture. To save money, buy the generic type instead of the name brand. Straight from the jar, peanut butter can cause birds a bit of a problem (you know how it sticks to the roof of your mouth), but adding cornmeal and seeds will create a tasty mixture to spread on tree bark or stuff into your special feeders.

Around Christmas, a decorative wreath feeder can be made for the birds. To a basic wreath, add sprays or seed clusters of milo, maize, wheat, millet, barley, or wild oats. Include dried seed pods, acorn caps, and pine cones that can be stuffed with your birdseed cake mixtures (either suet or peanut butter). For color and variety include berries, such as the red pyracantha. The finished wreath will add a festive touch to your winter feeding stations as well as provide food for the birds.

A water source is the last item needed for a winter feeding station, and something as simple as a garbage-can lid can be used to provide it. The lid can be attached to a stump, laid on a couple of cement blocks, or placed on the ground. However, if cats are a problem, it should be hung from a tree limb or clothesline. Drill three equally spaced holes just under the rim of the lid. Attach three ropes or cords and hang it high enough off the ground to protect the birds.

A well-maintained winter feeding station should meet the needs of your backyard birds until spring and give you many hours of bird-watching pleasure. If you want to continue to provide for the birds year-round, you might consider planting bushes, flowers, and trees that will provide not only seeds, berries, and insects for them to eat, but also nesting cover and shelter.

Some trees with edible berries, a few of which might be suitable for your area, are mulberry, dogwood, hawthorn, chokecherry, basswood, hackberry, and cedar. Shrubs and vines include yaupon, holly, pyracantha, Japanese privet, bayberry, members of the honeysuckle family, bittersweet, and Virginia creeper. You can plant any kind of flower since all of them have some kind of seed that may appeal to visiting birds. However, if possible, include the sunflower, as it is a special favorite.

When you have provided a feeding station for the birds' winter needs and planted growing things for their year-round use, sit back and enjoy watching the different species that visit your backyard sanctuary.

Around Christmas, a decorative wreath feeder can be made for the birds.

Bluebirds

Severe weather, destruction of nesting habitat, and heavy competition with sparrows and starlings have caused a decline in the nation's bluebird population. Although the pressure is not as drastic in Texas as in the North and East, this beautiful member of the thrush family needs a helping hand. Three species of bluebirds — eastern, western, and mountain — make their homes in Texas during various times of the year. All of them are close in size, 6-1/2 to 7-1/2 inches, and weigh about one ounce.

Most common and widespread is the eastern bluebird, *Sialia sialis.* Although it is considered a partial migrant, it winters throughout most of Texas, except the Trans-Pecos. Almost anywhere, except the treeless prairies and heavily wooded forests, is suitable to this particular bird's needs.

The male has a bright blue back, rusty breast and throat, and white belly and undertail area. Its beautiful coloring caused the famous American writer Henry David Thoreau to say that the bird carries the sky on its back. American naturalist John Burrows observed that it also has the warm reddish-brown of the earth on its breast. Coloration of the female is much duller and paler. The young, unlike adults, have mouse-gray backs and the white speckled breasts so characteristic of thrushes. Only while they are young do these birds display their relationship to the thrush family in their coloration. A tinge of dull blue in the wings and tail give a hint of the bright colors they will wear one day.

When perching, this species appears dumpy and round-shouldered. Flight is considered more or less irregular unless the bird is traveling long distances. Short flights usually are not at a great height. During courtship the male ascends fifty to one hundred feet and then floats down to flutter around the female. He may even offer her food as he woos her with songs and tries to convince her to examine the nest site he has chosen. Finally she flies into the cavity and accepts it and the male. After lining it with grass, she lays four to six light blue eggs. Most, if not all, of the incubation during the required twelve-day period is done by the female. Both parents feed the nestlings, but again, the female does the larger share. However, when the young become fledglings and are able to leave the nest, the male takes over so the female can prepare the nest for a second brood. The male continues to feed the fledglings while teaching them to feed themselves. Sometimes young from the first brood help the parents feed the second brood.

About three-fourths of bluebirds' diet consists of insects such as beetles, grasshoppers, and caterpillars. Berries and other fruit make up the rest of their menu. Food preferences make the bluebird one of those species considered beneficial to people.

The western bluebird, *Sialia mexicana,* is very similar to the eastern except the male's throat is blue and he has a rusty patch on his back. Females are duller than the males and have a whitish throat. This species winters in the Trans-Pecos and breeds in the Guadalupe Mountains.

Except for its whitish belly, the mountain bluebird, *Sialis currucoides,* is a beautiful turquoise blue. No red appears on either the male or the female. In fall and winter the male's plumage shows touches of dull brown, which is the predominant year-round color of the female. Her drab coloring is relieved only by bluish markings on her rump, tail, and wings. The mountain bluebird, which winters in the western two-thirds of Texas, has a straighter,

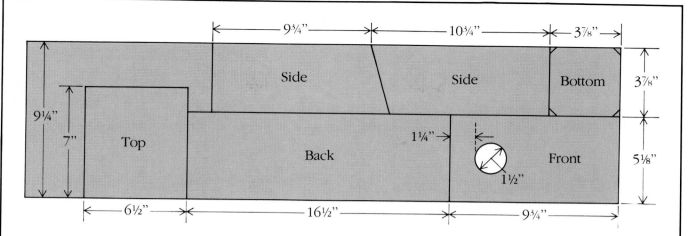

Build a Bluebird House

Materials List

1. 1 x 10-inch lumber—33 inches.
2. 6½ inches of ½-inch wood dowel or metal hinge.
3. One 1½-inch wood screw with washer.
4. 20 to 25 1½ to 1¾-inch nails.
5. Wire or ring-shank nails to attach box to post.

Construction Notes

1. Dimensions given are for ¾-inch thick lumber.
2. Make entrance hole precisely 1½ inches in diameter and 1¼ inches from the top.
3. Provide space between top and sides for ventilation.
4. If possible, use 1¾-inch galvanized siding nails or aluminum nails.
5. Round corners on bottom of box for drainage, and recess bottom ¼-inch.
6. Roughen inside of front board by making notches with a saw or holes with an awl or drill, to assist young in climbing to entrance hole.
7. Top of the box should be attached at the back by a ½-inch wooden dowel or metal hinge, and in front by a 1½-inch wood screw to facilitate easy opening for inspection and cleaning.
8. Drill two or three holes in the back panel of the box above and below the enclosure, to aid in quick, easy attachment to pole or post.
9. Do not add any type of perch to the box; it will only serve to attract sparrows.

Site Selection

Site selection is the single most important step in having a successful bluebird program. Bluebirds utilize only a very specific type of habitat for nesting and only rarely will deviate from it. In general, bluebirds prefer open areas with scattered trees where the ground is not covered with tall undergrowth.

There are three general areas that should be avoided when selecting a nest site:

1. Avoid placing nest boxes in towns or within the immediate area of farm yards. House sparrows invariably will occupy every such nest box.
2. Do not place boxes in heavy timber. Bluebirds prefer sites associated with timber, but more at the edge of a clearing rather than in the timber stand itself.
3. Do not place boxes in or near areas of widespread insecticide use. Bluebirds feed almost entirely on insects during the nesting season.

Installation and Maintenance

1. Place boxes at 150 to 200-yard intervals.
2. Mount boxes about five to seven feet above ground level. Fence posts make excellent mounting sites.
3. Clean boxes as soon as possible after a successful hatch. Bluebirds will not utilize the same nest box unless it is cleaned.

less hunched posture than the other bluebirds.

All species of bluebirds are cavity nesters, which means they nest in holes in trees, shrubs, fence posts, and birdhouses. With a bit of interior remodeling, they can convert abandoned woodpecker holes into comfortable nests. Chip-strewn floors may be all right for hardy woodpeckers, but a soft grass lining must be added for the more delicate young bluebirds.

At one time there were plenty of natural nesting sites for the "blue robin," a name given the bird by early settlers because of its reddish breast. Its preference for sites bordering open areas was met as the pioneers cleared forest lands for farming. The holes in the posts and rails of the wooden fences they built provided additional nesting places and the bluebird's population grew.

Their first efforts benefited the bird, but later actions were not so kind. When early settlers imported the English house sparrow and the European starling, both cavity nesting birds, they brought to America two species that are in direct competition with the bluebird for available nesting sites. Since sparrows and starlings are extremely aggressive, the gentle bluebird often lost out to its foreign competitors. Non-migrating sparrows contested the bluebird's rights to live in cities and towns in their northern range by being well established in all available housing when the bluebirds returned from their southern migration. There was nothing the bluebirds could do but move to the country. Fortunately for them, sparrows seldom use abandoned woodpecker holes or natural cavities in decaying trees as homes.

Changing life-styles also brought problems for the bluebird. As small farms were consolidated into larger, more profitable agricultural complexes, thousands of miles of hole-riddled wooden fences were eliminated. Metal fence posts often replaced wooden ones that had provided nest sites along our roadsides. Invention of the chainsaw did not help the bluebird either. These efficient machines made it possible for landowners to cut down old, unsightly, cavity-filled trees from pastures and fencerows, thereby removing natural bluebird housing.

Severe weather also takes its toll of the brightly colored birds. Although the bluebird is an early migrant, it is not a hardy bird. Prematurely warm weather may draw flocks of them north too soon, and then they freeze when cold weather returns.

With everything working against them, it is a wonder there are any bluebirds left at all. Noticing a decline in the birds' numbers, concerned conservationists launched several campaigns to provide artificial housing for the birds. Results have been very good, especially when the houses have been placed outside the city limits or in parks. In some areas, bluebird trails have been established on rural roads. The bluebird houses are attached to fence posts or trees and spaced no closer than 200 feet nor more than a half-mile apart along the roads for miles. One man in Illinois in one season put 102 houses along 43 miles of road near his home. The world's longest bluebird trail stretches through Manitoba and Saskatchewan in Canada. Its 7,000 nesting boxes cover about 2,000 miles of roadways. More than 8,000 young bluebirds and 15,000 tree swallows, a species which also finds bluebird houses to its liking, were raised in these Canadian nests in one year.

When bluebirds are present, they adapt quickly to the artificial nesting cavities and even seem to prefer them to natural ones. For those of you who would like to help the bluebirds, here are some instructions for building their houses. Whether the house design is plain or fancy makes no difference to the birds, but there are some basic requirements that must be met.

First, and very important, is the size of the entrance hole. It should be no larger than 1-1/2 inches in diameter and should be located so the lower edge of the hole is between 4 and 5-1/2 inches from the bottom of the house. If the hole is smaller than the prescribed size, the bluebird cannot enter. If the hole is placed too low, there isn't enough space below it for nesting material; however, a hole placed too high could prevent the nestlings from reaching the opening to the world of flight. No perch or landing platform should be attached beneath the entrance hole. Such accessories attract sparrows and discourage bluebirds.

Floor space may vary from an eight-inch square to a less spacious four-inch square. Trim off the four corners slightly or drill a half-inch hole in each one to provide floor drainage. Recommended side height is eight inches, but it can be taller as long as the entrance hole spacing is correct. For ventilation, drill four one-fourth-inch holes in each side about an inch below the roofline, or allow the sides to be one-fourth inch shorter than the front and back to create a crack between the roof and sides. The front, roof, or bottom should be hinged in some manner so the house can be cleaned before each nesting season. The house should not be cleaned between the first and second brood in one season. Color has little to do with acceptance or rejection by nesters, but if paint or stain is applied, it should be confined to the outside. Hot sun and treated interiors can combine to create noxious fumes capable of killing nestlings.

Bluebird houses should be hung so they will not swing in the breeze. For best results, attach them firmly to a post or tree at least five feet from the ground in open areas. Bluebirds nest successfully in old fence posts at heights of two or three feet, but they are not as likely to attract predators in these natural cavities as in man-made houses because their fence posts look like hundreds of other unoccupied fence posts. To prevent climbing predators from reaching the nest, it may be necessary to add a metal shield below the house. Greased metal poles also help to discourage predators. Wherever you put your birdhouse, make sure no overhanging branches or foliage prevent the birds from flying directly to the entrance. Some birders insist that the entrance face south, but others claim the house may face any point on the compass.

Although the 1-1/2-inch entrance hole excludes starlings, sparrows have no trouble entering. If a sparrow lays claim to your bluebird house before a bluebird is attracted, remove the sparrow's nest as quickly as it is built. This may have to be repeated several times before the nesting sparrow gives up and moves to another location. Only with your help will the mild-mannered bluebird be able to compete with the sparrow. Your efforts, whether you build one or a dozen bluebird houses, will help this bird compete for nesting space. Wouldn't it be tragic if the lack of housing wiped this beautiful songbird from the face of the earth?

Both parents feed the bluebird babies, until the young fledglings leave the nest.

Cardinals and Pyrrhuloxias

It would be difficult to mistake the male cardinal for any other North American bird. His bright red feathers, distinct head crest, and black mask and throat patch set him apart from all the rest. He is a welcome resident throughout the United States, and his popularity has earned him the distinction of being the state bird for Illinois, Ohio, Kentucky, Virginia, West Virginia, and North Carolina. Audubon declared, "In richness of plumage, elegance of motion and strength of song, this species surpasses all its kindred in the United States."

The female cardinal did not receive an equal measure of flamboyant good looks. She has the distinctive crest and red bill of the male, but her yellowish, cinnamon-brown plumage contains only touches of red. One birder described her as looking as if she were wearing an ashy-brown chiffon veil over a rose dress. This "chiffon veil" might also be thought of as a camouflage suit, which allows her and her young to hide from predators. Unlike the females in most species, she is an accomplished vocalist and may be heard singing along with the male. Many admirers believe her song more than makes up for her drab appearance.

The soft warbling of young cardinals, quite unlike the adult vocalizations, does not begin to contain adult sounds until the young are about two months old. At first the crested fledglings are even duller and browner than their mother. As time passes, their blackish bills slowly lighten, going through stages of purple and raspberry before finally becoming red. Their short, stubby tail feathers lengthen, and by the time the young have their first winter plumage, they look like their parents.

A close relative of the cardinal, which the less observant person may mistake for a female cardinal, is the pyrrhuloxia (pir-ah-LOX-see-ah). This bird has the same conspicuous crest, but its bill is yellow, and it has gray plumage tinged with red. The crest, mask, throat, chest, tail, and wing tips of the male are highlighted with obvious red. When the pyrrhuloxia's crest is flattened, its short curved bill and round head give it the bored look of a caged parrot. However, when the crest is raised to its full height and thrown forward, the bird becomes the picture of alertness. The female pyrrhuloxia is mostly grayish brown with a touch of red in her crest, wings, and tail. The young resemble her, but they have lighter underparts and a dusky-colored bill.

Southwestern deserts and plains are home to pyrrhuloxias. In Texas they live in the arid Brush Country, preferring a thorny scrub of mesquite, cactus, acacia, and yucca to the bushes, shrubs, trees, and backyard habitats of the cardinal. No interbreeding of the two species occurs, even in areas where their ranges overlap.

Pyrrhuloxias congregate in large feeding flocks during the winter. On rare occasion a flock may contain as many as one thousand birds. When these winter flocks break up, the competition for nesting territories begins. It is not unusual to find the female helping her mate chase off the competition. Once the couple has established its territorial boundaries, the female selects a thorny thicket in which to construct her cuplike nest, composed of strips of bark, grasses, and twigs. She lines it with fine grasses and other vegetable fibers before laying her three to four eggs. Their white shells are marked with shades of dark brown and purplish gray.

Cardinals also gather in sociable groups during the winter, but these

Female cardinal

groups rarely contain more than twenty-five individual birds, with smaller groups the rule. Since they do not migrate, cardinals must sustain themselves on whatever is available, regardless of the weather. For this reason, they are common visitors to backyard feeding stations and offer hours of watching enjoyment to those who cater to their needs.

The male cardinal is an aggressive defender of his home territory and quick to attack any trespassers when spring boundaries are being established. So highly developed is this aggression that male cardinals have been observed fighting their own reflections in mirrors, window panes, hubcaps, and bumpers. They will go so far as to attack red objects.

Once the territorial claims are established, the female is attracted and courted by song. She then selects a dense tangle of vegetation in a thicket or patch of shrubbery as a nest site. Her nest, similar to that of the pyrrhuloxia, will hold three or four greenish or bluish white eggs spotted with reddish brown. During the two weeks she incubates the eggs, the male cardinal feeds

Cardinals and Pyrrhuloxias **29**

Male cardinal

Male pyrrhuloxia

Female pyrrhuloxia

her. When the eggs hatch, his duties are far from over. He helps the female gather food for the nestlings, and when they become fledglings, he takes over their care and feeding so the female can start a second brood. Cardinals are enthusiastic breeders and occasionally will raise as many as three broods in a single nesting season. The parents and their broods often stay together throughout the winter season.

Female cardinals and their young are more secretive in their habits than the male. Much of their time is spent in the thick tangles of brush. The male prefers an open perch high above the ground where he can sing to all the world. According to Harry C. Oberholser's book *The Bird Life of Texas*, the call note of the cardinal is a sharp, emphatic *tchip* or *whit*. His song is loud, clear, rich, variable whistles, usually sustained and distinctly phrased: *Hew, hew, hew hew hew hew* or *what-cheer, hew hew hew* or *hew, whoit whoit whoit whoit*. The female sings more softly and somewhat less frequently than the male.

The pyrrhuloxia's call note is a sharp, metallic *cheek*. His songs include a series of loud, metallic *quinks* and a thin, slurred *what-cheer, what-cheer,* etc. Both songs suggest the vocalizations of the cardinal, but neither is as long or as full and rich. Although female pyrrhuloxias are capable of song, they rarely sing.

The cardinal is delightful to hear and beautiful to see, but despite Audubon's description, it is not a graceful bird. Its flight is quick, jerky, and noisy. Perhaps for this reason it restricts its movements to short flights between bushes, trees, and the ground. Its quick, jerky flight is perfect for darting around in thick vegetation.

Cardinals and pyrrhuloxias will no doubt continue to confuse the casual observer. However, those who take the time to get to know them will be able to appreciate their subtle differences.

Woodpeckers

Repeatedly slamming your head against a tree would soon scramble your brains, but the woodpecker can do it as often as one hundred times a minute without any problems. The reason is that the woodpecker's body is perfectly designed for its unusual life-style. Let's examine this specialized body to see how the woodpecker can chip its way into almost any type of wood from morning to night.

Strong neck muscles provide the force behind the blow that drives the straight, hard, chisel-pointed beak into the wood. Since the head must take the impact of each stroke, the bones between the beak and the thick skull are not rigidly joined as they are in most other birds. A spongy, elastic tissue connects these flexible joints and acts as a shock absorber. Bristly feathers around the nostrils help filter out the wood dust created as the woodpecker pounds away.

Short, powerful legs connect the body to feet that can grip the side of any tree with ease. In most woodpecker species, the foot has four toes with sharply pointed, curved claws. These toes are arranged so two point to the front and two to the back. This gives the bird a firm, tonglike grip. (The three-toed species, which have only one toe pointed to the back, also manage a firm grip.)

Stiff tail feathers act as a prop to brace and steady the bird as it works. The very tips of these feathers seem to be almost elastic as they bend and spread into every tiny crack or crevice to give support on a smooth-surfaced tree or pole. The woodpecker's need for these stiff tail feathers is emphasized by its method of molting (feather replacement). The two middle feathers, which usually are quite strong and serve as the bird's main props, do not fall out until the other ten tail feathers have been re-

placed and once again can support the bird.

Woodpecker tongues are even more specialized, with each species having distinctive features designed for its own particular feeding requirements. In general, their tongues are long and can be extended beyond the tip of the bill. (This may not seem unusual to you, but in the bird world, only woodpeckers and hummingbirds can extend their tongues.) Most of their tongue tips are armed with backward-projecting spines or barbs that are used to impale wood-boring insects, making them easier to remove from their hidden tunnels.

The sapsucker, a member of the woodpecker family that gets its name from feeding mainly on tree sap, has no need to extend its tongue into the tree to catch insects. In place of the usual long, barbed tongue, it has a shorter tongue bristling with hairs at the tip. These hairs form a brushlike instrument just perfect for licking up sap and the occasional insect drawn to the oozing liquid.

The flicker is found on the ground more often than other woodpeckers because it feeds there. Its extra-long tongue has few barbs, but it is specially adapted for lapping up ants, a major food item for the bird. Large salivary glands on each side of its mouth secrete a sticky mucous coating for the tongue. When the flicker extends its long tongue into an anthill or along a well-traveled ant trail, the insects rush to attack what looks like an invading worm. They are caught by the sticky mucus and are quickly eaten.

But where does the flicker put such a long tongue when it is not extended catching ants? The tongue is divided into two branches at the rear, but instead of being attached to the bottom of the skull as in most birds, these branches pass on either side of the windpipe. Lengthened by two bony ligaments, they slide up over the skull (beneath the skin, of course), come together at the forehead and extend down into the right nostril. As easily as a knife slips in and out of its sheath, the woodpecker's tongue glides smoothly along its path over the skull as the bird flicks it in and out while feeding. Depending upon the species of woodpecker, the back of the tongue ends at the base of the bill, in the upper beak, or, rarely, behind or below the eye. In any case, the woodpecker has part of its tongue on top of its head.

The woodpecker's strong beak and barbed tongue are a great combination for getting rid of insect pests living beneath the tree bark. However, without its excellent hearing, the bird would not be very good at locating its prey. The evidence of this can be seen in the following account by a forester. "I once saw a pileated woodpecker fly to a tough old hickory tree in which ants were using a little knothole as their entrance. The bird didn't drill in this obvious place. Instead, it circled the trunk, gently tapping, then pausing. Finally it proceeded to whack into the very heart of the ant nest—five feet below the knothole."

We do not know whether the bird heard the movements of the disturbed insects or was able to distinguish subtle differences in the tapping sound caused by the ants' hollowed-out tunnels and nest. However, we do know that something pinpointed the spot where further investigation was needed and, since the bird cannot boast x-ray vision, it is fairly safe to assume that the woodpecker's hearing played a major role in locating the ant nest.

Some people believe all woodpeckers are destructive pests because they chip holes into trees looking for food. But by stripping the bark from a dead

The pileated woodpecker, largest woodpecker in the United States.

The aptly named red-headed wood-pecker.

or dying tree and eliminating the resident populations of carpenter ants or wood-boring grubs and insects, the woodpecker actually helps to prevent the spread of these destructive creatures to healthy trees nearby.

The story is told of a man who awoke one morning to find a woodpecker hammering away at his favorite oak tree. Thinking that he was protecting the tree, he chased away the bird and covered the riddled part of the tree trunk with wire mesh. Bright and early the next morning the bird was back. Persistent pecking reduced the wire mesh to tatters and the bird resumed its drilling into the oak. The man continued to harass the bird until the woodpecker finally gave up and flew away. The man congratulated himself for saving his prized oak from the bird. Time, however, proved him wrong. A few years later, during a severe storm, the tree trunk snapped at the spot where the woodpecker had been drilling. An examination revealed that a colony of carpenter ants had riddled the seemingly healthy tree with a maze of galleries and tunnels. If the woodpecker had been allowed to continue its drilling, the ant nest probably would have been eradicated and the tree saved from the unseen destruction lurking within.

In addition to the wood-chiseling activities associated with feeding, all woodpeckers use their beaks to chip out a nesting cavity of some type in a tree, stump, telephone pole, fence post, or other such wooden object. Their white, unmarked eggs are laid on a bed of wood chips and splinters in the bottom of the cavity. Both parents feed the young, pumping them full of predigested food until they are able to forage for themselves.

Other than a rattling, cackling call, which can hardly be called singing, woodpeckers communicate with each other by drumming. The sound is made by rapidly striking the beak against a hollow tree trunk, dead branch, tin roof, garbage can lid, or other resonant object. This drumming serves as a warning to territorial trespassers and is used to attract a mate.

When one woodpecker's drumming was analyzed with special recording equipment, it was discovered that the bird produced 500 to 600 two-second bursts of sound a day. Each two-second burst contained as many as forty rapid blows. In some species the tapping is so varied it sounds like a complicated code. These tapped conversations take place between the male and female throughout the courting and nesting. Each coming and going from the nest is accompanied by the proper number and sequence of strokes.

The next time you hear a woodpecker's jackhammerlike blows you will know it is either talking, feeding, or building a home. Whichever the bird is doing, it is filling its niche in the woodland environment.

Killdeer

Widespread, numerous, and noisy—these words describe the killdeer, *Charadrius vociferus*, a conspicuous, easy-to-identify member of the plover family. It is one of the noisiest of American birds, which accounts for the "vociferus" part of its scientific name. Although the killdeer is classed as a migratory species, this bird is a year-round resident of Texas, choosing a variety of habitats as home. It is found throughout the state, with the possible exception of the Panhandle during frigid winter weather. It thrives in open or semiopen areas and is at home in either dry or wet locations. An arid mesa or canyon can be as appealing as a home near a river or by a lakeshore. Plains and prairies, whether grassy or bare, and fields or pastures, whether cultivated or fallow, attract the birds as often as the marshes, beaches, bays, and lagoon flats of the coast. Killdeer also manage to live side-by-side with people, using airports, golf courses, and lawns as foraging areas. Pebbled rooftops serve as well for nest sites as dry gravel beds along creeks and rivers.

When spring rolls around, the birds pair off to search for a nesting site. An ideal one, of course, would be near water, but the birds are adaptable and manage under less-than-ideal conditions. After choosing the best possible location, they find a shallow depression that can be lined with bits of grass, weeds, bark, shells, or rocks to form a crude nest. The building materials selected from the area help the nest blend into the surroundings. The female then lays four light buff or chocolate-colored eggs, blotched with black and dark brown spots.

Both nest and eggs blend into the surroundings, but the birds take no chances, guarding the nest constantly throughout the twenty-six- to twenty-eight-day incubation period. If the nest

A mother killdeer sits on her nest, which is little more than a shallow depression.

Killdeer chicks and a remaining egg lie in their nest of lined rocks.

is threatened, the female is a master at the art of subterfuge. Imitating a severely injured bird, she flutters a few feet from the nest, falls flat on the ground as though hopelessly wounded, and utters piteous cries. If approached, she recovers enough to move farther from the nest, but continues to drag one or both wings on the ground as if broken. She may even roll over and gasp and pant as if completely exhausted by her efforts. Throughout the performance she continues to cry pitifully as if in pain. By spreading her tail feathers and throwing her body from side to side, she exposes a golden-red rump patch that may look like blood to the enemy. The male also may get into the act, flying around the intruder at a safe distance, screaming protests. Working as a team, they continue the performance until the intruder is lured away from the nest.

Another diversion the birds use is the false nest act. When feeding birds

The female killdeer is quite an actress when her nest is threatened.

are approached, one will move away, completely ignoring the enemy, and settle into a depression with all the motions associated with covering a nest of eggs. As the enemy draws near, the bird glides off to expose the empty depression. To add insult, the bird also makes a cry that sounds like a chuckle. If the enemy continues to follow, the false nest act will be repeated until the follower gets tired of looking into empty depressions and goes away.

Once the eggs hatch, the parents must transfer their protection to the young, which follow them around on long, slender legs. At the first cry of alarm, the chicks flatten themselves on the ground with their necks outstretched. Motionless, they blend into their surroundings and seem to disappear. Instinctively they seem to realize that the slightest movement could be their last. They remain in this motionless position until their parents return and voice an all-clear signal.

If a curious animal that appears to offer no threat to the birds happens into the area, killdeer may gang up on it. The first one to spot it will fly almost

into the animal's face while uttering loud, shrill cries. This scolding attracts others who join in just as noisily as the first. The intruder usually is intimidated by this display and retreats to more pleasant surroundings. These noisy outcries also alert other birds in the area to the presence of possible danger.

The flight of the killdeer is swift but erratic, and it seldom flies for long periods. While on the ground, the bird usually walks, but it can run with astonishing speed. When feeding, the bird runs four or five steps, stops, bobs, takes a few more steps, stops, and bobs again. At each stop, it raises its head high and checks its surroundings. This vertical movement of its head and the flashing of its black and white throat bands may startle insects into moving and betraying their location to the feeding bird. A quick jab of the beak may capture a beetle, grasshopper, earthworm, snail, spider, or even a few seeds. Its control of many insect pests makes the killdeer a beneficial bird to have around, and its antics make it an entertaining bird to watch.

Owls

Since ancient times, the poor owl has been associated with bad omens by many people. Our literature is filled with such descriptions as "messenger of death," "harbinger of evil," and "bird of witchcraft." Even in biblical references the owl is listed as an abomination among the fowls (Leviticus) and figures prominently in scenes of destruction and ruination. Isaiah used the owl as a symbol of misery, desolation, and decay: "And thorns shall come up in her palaces; nettles and brambles in the fortresses thereof; and it shall be an habitation of dragons, and a court for owls."

On the other hand, not all images are unfavorable to the bird. The owl has frequently been associated with the gods and was the special bird of Minerva, Goddess of War and Wisdom of the Romans. When writing of the defeat of the Persians, Aristophanes said:

Yet we drove their ranks before us,
　ere the fall of eventide,
As we closed, an owl flew o'er us, and
　the gods were on our side.

Sir Philip Sidney, in his "Remedy for Love," wrote: "O you virtuous owle, / The wise Minerva's only fowle."

Owls are often portrayed as having wisdom, as in the following anonymous rhyme:

A wise old owl sat in an oak,
The more he saw the less he spoke,
The less he spoke the more he heard,
Why can't we all be like that wise old bird.

In reality the owl possesses no supernatural powers or exceptional wisdom, but it is probably the most effective mousetrap around. Owls are primarily birds of the twilight and night, although some species are diurnal, hunting during the day. Under severe press of hunger or when demanding owlets are in the nest, nocturnal species also may hunt during the day, especially when the day is cloudy or heavily overcast. Nature has well equipped the owl for its particular role in life. Its whole body is designed to make it an efficient and deadly night hunter.

First of all, the bird achieves almost noiseless flight and can swoop down on its victim unheard. Two factors work together to accomplish this. First, large wings and a light body enable the owl to support itself easily and quietly in flight. A heavy-bodied bird requires hard-working wings that tend to be noisy. If you have ever heard a startled quail take flight, you have some idea of the noise some birds' wings can make. Second, most owls' feathers are finely fringed on the edges and covered with a velvetlike pile to help deaden the sound of air movement in flight. However, some, such as the pigmy owls, have hard plumage and their unmuffled wings are not noiseless. Since pigmy owls pounce on their prey from vantage points during the early morning and late afternoon, they do not need the silent flight required by the nocturnal species.

Another advantage nature has given the owl is excellent eyesight. An owl's eye is probably the most efficient organ of vision possesed by any animal. It has a visual sensitivity at least 35 times greater than ours, and possibly as much as 100 times greater. But the owl still cannot see in absolute darkness. Luckily, total darkness, except in deep cave systems, is very rare in nature. On a moonless, cloudy night, which appears to be pitch black to us, the actual level of illumination rarely drops below .004 foot candles. Studies have shown that the long-eared, tawny, and barn owls can see their prey from six feet away with as little as .00000073 foot candles of illumination. It is no

The barn owl's white, heart-shaped face, hunched back, and deep-set black eyes give it an almost ghostly look.

wonder that this fantastic night vision has given rise to so many folk tales of supernatural ability.

An owl's eyesight also is binocular, providing it with a single field of three-dimensional vision similar to that enjoyed by humans. Although the owl's eyeballs are not capable of rotary movement as ours are, the bird overcomes this drawback by having an extremely flexible neck, which enables it to rotate its head at least 180 degrees and possibly as much as 270 degrees. This ability accounts for the old tale that a person can walk circles around a nesting owl and cause it to twist off its head.

Exceptionally keen hearing completes the owl's nocturnal design. Some people have the mistaken idea that the tufts of feathers located on the tops of some owls' heads are ears. These "ear tufts" have nothing to do with the ears or the owl's hearing. They are merely elongated head feathers that can be erected or depressed at will, perhaps to communicate attack, withdrawal, or some other type of owl body language. They also aid the bird in its camouflage efforts. As the owl sits motionless in its alert posture, it looks like a broken upright tree stub, an illusion that is emphasized by the ear tufts.

Protruding external ears, which are so common to mammals, are not found in the bird world. That type of ear

Small burrowing owls like to take over the burrows of other animals.

Screech owls may display either a rufous (reddish or rusty brown) or a gray color phase.

would cause air resistance when the bird was in flight. The owl's actual ears are concealed behind the edges of its facial eye disks. These large ear openings look like concave dishes. By erecting or depressing the plumage in front of or behind the ear openings, the owl is able to direct its hearing in different directions.

In addition to being efficient receivers of sound, the owl's ears are especially tuned to high-frequency sounds, such as those made by squeaky-voiced rodents. Noises caused as the rodents scurry across dried vegetation, sticks, and other debris also contain a great number of high-frequency sounds that give the owl a clue to the whereabouts of its prey. Studies of barn owls have shown that this bird's excellent hearing enables it to catch living prey in absolute darkness if the rodent squeaks or rustles a leaf to give away its location.

Although rodents make up a large percentage of the owl's diet, they are not the only item on the menu. These efficient predators also eat insects, earthworms, fish, crayfish, amphibians, birds, and small animals. Food studies of owls can be quite accurate because the bird leaves an involuntary record of what it has eaten. Although an owl sometimes crushes the skull of a mouse or plucks the long wing and tail feathers from a bird, it swallows its prey whole when possible. Larger animals are torn into pieces that can be gulped down. Bones, feathers, fur, and entrails are all swallowed. The nourishing parts are digested and the indigestible parts are compressed into a pellet that is coughed up by the owl.

Owl pellets have proven quite valuable to professionals studying the relationship between predators and prey. There can be no doubt as to which prey species are being eaten by owls. Fossilized pellets also have provided us with

Owl pellets contain the indigestible remains of animals swallowed whole or in large pieces the night before.

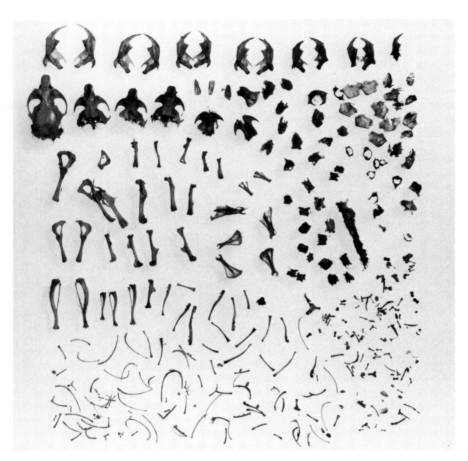

These bones, removed from one large owl pellet, indicate that this particular owl ate at least seven rodents during its previous night's hunt, and they ranged from large to small.

one of the few true records of what was actually eaten by animals long dead. If you happen to come across an owl pellet, you might want to do a bit of detective work on your own to determine what that particular bird ate. The best way to find out what the pellet contains is to soften it in water and then carefully take it apart. You might even want to examine the contents under a magnifying glass or microscope.

Almost everything about the owl is unusual and interesting. Take time to learn more about it and you will prob-ably agree that this feathered mouse-trap is usually beneficial.

Roadrunners, Cuckoos, and Anis

One of the strangest families in the bird world is the one that includes the roadrunner, cuckoos, and anis (AH-nees). In fact, the appearance, food habits, and other characteristics of these three species are so different it is hard to believe they belong to the same family. However, ornithologists (or-na-THAL-ah-jists), people who study birds, consider more than just outward appearances when they group birds. They recognize that despite their many differences, these birds also have many characteristics in common. All of them are slender birds with rounded wings, curved bills, and long floppy tails. Their tail feathers also are graduated in size, with the shortest ones on the outer edges, and the males and females within each species look alike. Another family trait can be seen in the tracks, which look like *X*'s. This strange track, which makes it hard to tell whether the birds are coming or going, occurs because their feet have two toes pointing forward and two pointing back. This arrangement enables them to climb and grasp.

The roadrunner and its track have inspired many beliefs and superstitions.

The roadrunner's running speed has been clocked at about fifteen miles per hour.

J. Frank Dobie, noted folklorist and perhaps the roadrunner's greatest fan, wrote that the Pueblo Indians of New Mexico drew the bird's track on the ground near the tent of their dead to mislead evil spirits trying to follow the departed soul. To ward off the henchmen of the "Bad God," Plains Indians often hung the whole skin of a roadrunner over their lodge door. The Tarahumare Indians of the Sierra Madre claimed their running skill was a result of eating meals that included roadrunner meat.

Luck, both good and bad, also has been attributed to the roadrunner. One of these birds living near a home brought the residents good fortune. One crossing the road from left to right brought good luck, but one crossing in the opposite direction brought bad luck. Early travelers also believed that if a lost man found and followed a roadrunner or its tracks, he would be led to a trail. Since the roadrunner is known to hunt for insects in the vegetation along roads, deer trails, and animal pathways, this belief has a basis in fact.

Speaking of food habits, the roadrunner will eat anything from insects to small mammals, as well as fruits, seeds, and prickly pear. The bird is particularly fond of lizards and snakes, including small rattlesnakes, and its method of killing them could be considered another unusual characteristic of the bird. To kill a snake, the roadrunner circles around it. Using speed, agility, and quick leaps into the air to stay clear of the snake's fangs, the bird rushes in and stabs the snake with its

The roadrunner's short, rounded wings allow it to glide to the ground from tree perches or leap into the air when startled.

pointed beak. Repeated blows stun the snake so it can be seized and slammed against the ground. The bird then pounds it repeatedly against the ground or a rock until the bones in the snake's head and body are broken or crushed. Lizards and other large prey also are killed and softened in this manner.

It is especially interesting to watch a nest-bound young being fed a snake brought by one of its parents. When the snake is too long, the parent forces as much of the reptile down the young one's gullet as possible, leaving the excess hanging outside its beak. As the young bird's digestive juices work on the swallowed portion, the remainder slowly works its way inside. In a matter of hours the entire snake is eaten. Adults also have been seen running around with partially swallowed snakes hanging out of their mouths.

The roadrunner, a favorite with many people, is somewhat of a tourist attraction in the Southwest. Also known as chaparral cock, ground cuckoo, or paisano, the roadrunner usually is found on the ground. It uses its wings to leap into the air when startled or to glide to the ground from perches. Its fitful flight is seldom long and usually consists of a spectacular leap into the air followed by a crashing dive into dense brush for concealment. The rest of the time the bird can be found running across the ground at speeds up to fifteen miles per hour.

Perhaps because of the well-known cartoon character constantly being chased by the coyote, most people picture this bird only in a desert-type habitat. However, the roadrunner is equally at home among the swamp-

The groove-billed ani is probably the least known member of the cuckoo family.

Found over most of the United States, the yellow-billed cuckoo is graceful and swift on the wing.

lands, tall pines, and magnolias of East Texas, the limestone outcroppings and brush of the Hill Country, and the mesquites and prickly pear of West Texas. All the bird needs is some bare ground with more or less scattered trees and bushes where it can walk around and catch food.

Its white eggs are laid in a nest of sticks hidden in a cactus, tree, or thorny bush. Young are raised on such delicacies as lizards, snakes, scorpions, and insects. For the first twelve days, as one parent guards the nest and young, the other one hunts. When the hunting adult approaches the nest with food, the guardian adult leaves to take

its place hunting. These duties are switched with each return trip until the time when the size and hunger of the young birds force both adults to hunt at the same time. After the young are about two weeks old, the adults seldom bring anything smaller than a young lizard as food. The young are able to leave the nest three weeks after hatching, but they stay close by so the adults can feed and train them for a while longer.

Moving along to the next members of this strange family, we come to the cuckoos. Most common of the three cuckoo species is the yellow-billed cuckoo, which nests throughout Texas

and is found over most of the United States. It can be recognized by the yellow lower mandible on its slightly curved bill and the large white spots on the underside of its dark tail feathers. Its body is dull brown above and white below with reddish wing coloration. Graceful and swift on the wing, the yellowbill slips quietly through its leafy habitat. Birders seldom see it on an exposed limb since it prefers to skulk in the leaves, searching for insects and caterpillars. Its favorite food is caterpillars, including the hairy species that most birds pass up. The hairy spines often coat the inside of the bird's stomach. Because they eat many of the caterpillars that damage trees, such as the tent caterpillar, cuckoos should be welcome guests in yards and orchards. They also eat locusts, beetles, bugs, grasshoppers, ants, wasps, an occasional frog or lizard, and wild fruits, such as raspberry, elderberry, and mulberry.

As its name implies, the less colorful black-billed cuckoo has a black bill. It also has a narrow, red eye-ring, but lacks the yellowbill's reddish coloration in its wings. The tail spots, found on the underside of its olive-brown tail, are much smaller than those of the yellowbill. Trying to spot the blackbill is more difficult than seeing the yellowbill since it is an even greater recluse. It prefers the dense woodlands along streams, ponds, and lakes, the dense borders of meadows and forests, or the deep thickets and groves of coastal prairies. Although the blackbill visits orchards and gardens, it still remains well hidden from interested observers as it migrates through the eastern and central portions of the state. It is as much of a caterpillar hunter as the yellowbill, but the blackbill also eats a variety of grasshoppers, crickets, beetles, other insects, spiders, and, occasionally, wild fruits.

Yellow-billed and black-billed cuckoos usually build nests of twigs in bushes and trees and raise their own young. However, in areas where both are found, they may lay eggs in each other's nests. Occasionally the blackbill lays its eggs in the nests of other smaller woodland birds. This act, known as social parasitism, is a common practice among the Old World cuckoos. When the young cuckoo hatches, it usually pushes nest mates or unhatched eggs belonging to the foster parents out of the nest to make more room for itself. Foster parents may have a difficult time gathering enough food for their hungry, substitute offspring, which may be larger than they are.

The third member of this species, the rare mangrove cuckoo, does not make its home in Texas. In fact there has been only one recorded Texas sighting, back in 1964 on a Christmas bird count. This bird makes its home among the mangroves of the Florida Keys and along the southwest coast of Florida north to Tampa Bay. It also inhabits the West Indies, the mangrove belts of the lowlands in Middle America, the north coast of South America, and many offshore islands. It has bright buffy underparts and a black mask.

Because their chuckling call is heard most frequently on cloudy days, cuckoos are called "rain crows" by many people.

The groove-billed ani of South Texas and the smooth-billed ani of southern Florida are probably the least known members of this family and the oddest. They could easily be mistaken for blackbirds or grackles if it were not for their high, puffinlike beaks. As their name indicates, the groove-billed ani has grooves on its bill that are visible at close range, and the smooth-billed ani has none. In Texas, the birds stay in the thickest thornbrush they can find, choosing patches of Texas ebony, mesquite, huisache, and retama bushes. However, in Mexico and Central America these birds seem to be more at home in open pastures with only scattered bushes. Here they may be found in small flocks on the ground eating insects. They have learned to feed around the feet of grazing livestock, catching the insects disturbed by the cattle's hooves as they move about. Many insects can be found in this manner without too much effort on the part of the birds. Although anis eat mainly insects and an occasional lizard, they also will eat fruit, berries, and other vegetation, especially during the dry season. Their reputation as tick-eaters is grossly exaggerated, but they do perch on cattle and eat some ticks from the animals.

Anis are weak fliers, and it is funny to watch them flutter around in a strong wind. To take flight, the ani leaps into the air, gives a few quick flaps, sails for a couple of feet, flaps some more, and then sails again. When the bird lands, its tail flops forward over its back and almost knocks it off its perch. Despite its reputation as a weak flier and a resident of the tropics, the groove-billed ani has made startling appearances in such nontropical spots as Minnesota, Nebraska, and Kansas.

When nesting, the anis may follow the normal pattern of one pair of birds to one nest, or they may share a communal nest. In the latter method, two or more female anis lay their pale greenish blue eggs in the same untidy basket of twigs, leaves, and grass hidden in a thorny bush and then take turns incubating them. When the young hatch, all adults, males and females alike, share the task of feeding them. Some baby birds are considered cute, but the young ani with its black skin and huge bill can hardly qualify as appealing.

Even though the roadrunners, cuckoos, and anis would never win a "most beautiful" contest, they all could qualify for "personality" or "most unusual" awards. So the next time you laugh at the antics of a roadrunner, hear the *cuc-cuc-cuc* of the rain crow, or catch a glimpse of the ani, you will know that you have had a chance to meet a member of the unique Cuculidae family.

Doves and Pigeons

Completely different images come to mind when we hear the words pigeons and doves, but technically no difference exists between the two, and the terms often are used interchangeably. True, those small, fast-flying game birds, able to challenge the shooting skill of any bird hunter, are doves. However, that plump pigeon perched on a building ledge or waddling around the city park looking for a handout is also a dove—a rock dove.

All pigeons and doves are members of the Columbidae family. They have soft, thick plumage in a variety of colors and patterns, with most species displaying some type of iridescent glossing. No seasonal changes in coloration occur, and except for the somewhat duller hues of the female, the sexes are alike.

Both sexes share in incubating the eggs and in feeding the newly hatched young a substance called "pigeon milk," which is secreted from the adult's crop. Later the parents regurgitate partially digested food for the young. Adults eat seeds, fruit, and vegetable matter, and a few species also eat a variety of insects and other small invertebrates. Instead of drinking in the typical bird manner—taking a sip, tipping back the head, and allowing the water to trickle down the throat—the pigeon or dove immerses its bill and drinks with sustained sucking.

Of the 289 dove species found in the world, only 8 are considered full-time or part-time residents of Texas. Of these, only the mourning, white-winged, and white-tipped (white-fronted) doves are legal game birds.

The mourning dove, slightly smaller than the whitewing, is the most common and abundant game bird in the United States. It breeds in each of the contiguous forty-eight states and is the only native Texas bird that occurs in all of the state's 254 counties. As long as there is enough water present to allow the bird to drink once a day, the mourning dove can thrive in almost any habitat. This adaptive ability and its year-round multiple-nesting cycle contribute to its abundant numbers. Millions are harvested each year without endangering the population. Its cruising speed of forty miles per hour has enabled it to avoid many a shotgun blast and tests the skill of any bird hunter. When flights of mourning doves and whitewings mix, the mourning dove can be distinguished by its more rapid wing beat, erratic flight path, and pointed tail. Its mournful *ooah, cooo, cooo, coo* call is made year-round, and from a distance only the three *coo*'s can be heard.

The white-winged dove has a conspicuous white bar on its wings and a long, moderately rounded tail. This popular game bird generally is found south of a line extending from El Paso to Del Rio to San Antonio to Corpus Christi, with the heaviest concentrations in Starr, Cameron, Hidalgo, and Willacy counties. An isolated population is found on Galveston Island, and wandering birds occasionally may be spotted throughout the state in the fall.

Migrating whitewings begin moving into the Lower Rio Grande Valley at the end of March and set up housekeeping in native brush and citrus trees. Their adaptation to citrus trees is helping to counteract some of the losses brought about by the destruction of native brush in the area. Their call, which sounds something like the crowing of a young rooster, is made up of two vocalizations—a harsh *coo-uh-CUCK-oo* and a "*who-cooks-for-you*" sound.

The white-tipped dove, formerly known as the white-fronted dove, is similar in size and shape to the whitewing and may be mistaken for this

The small Inca dove adapts readily to urban areas and city parks.

game bird. However, the whitetip is slightly larger and has cinnamon-colored wing linings. Generally no more than one or two of these solitary birds are seen at a time. A local name for the whitetip is "jug blower" because its call is similar to the song made by blowing across the mouth of an empty bottle or jug.

Another characteristic that may help distinguish the whitetip from the whitewing is its tendency to fly less than ten feet off the ground. It appears to dislike flying and usually takes to the air only when startled. Despite its heavy body and ground-dwelling habits, its flight is swift when it heads for dense cover. Seldom is it seen above the tree tops, where the whitewings fly, but

hunters have to be sure of their targets when hunting around brush or citrus groves, as both species are common to these habitats and harvest limits are specific.

The white-tipped dove has adapted so well to the citrus orchards and urban areas that it has had a dramatic population increase during the last decade. Other than citrus orchards, the whitetip also makes its home in the shady woodlands and river thickets, seeking the densest brush it can find. It is difficult to observe because of its rather secretive habits and preference for dense thickets.

Although the increase in population has slightly expanded the whitetip's range, the lower portion of Texas is still the only place in the United States where it resides. It is classed as a migratory species under the Migratory Bird Treaty Act, but the Texas population is migratory only because some fly back and forth across the Rio Grande. Most spend their lives within a three-mile radius, and they prefer to walk instead of fly.

During the 1984–85 dove season, the white-tipped dove (white-fronted dove) became a legal game bird in Texas. It has been hunted for years in Mexico, but until data from studies conducted in Texas indicated it could be hunted in limited numbers without adversely affecting the breeding population, it enjoyed protected status.

Rock doves, commonly called domestic pigeons, need no introduction to city dwellers. These twelve- to thirteen-inch birds are extremely variable in color and pattern, ranging from gray to brown to all white with every combination of the three and occasional black markings. All display a white rump patch. Except when the weather is extremely hot or cold, the rock dove's distinctive *oo-roo-coo* or

coo-roo-coo call can be heard year-round.

Their dependence upon handouts in the city and their habit of eating cattle and chicken feed in rural areas make the rock doves seem quite domestic. Few people consider them true wild birds. They generally fly in flocks and do not readily mix with other wild birds. The rock dove has been introduced into almost all parts of the world, and individuals often raise them, as well as other varieties of racing and fancy pigeons.

About half the size of a mourning dove, the small Inca dove has an overall scaly appearance and a long tail with white margins. It displays strong domestic tendencies, choosing to live near humans. It adapts readily to urban areas and city parks and seems to be as much at home eating livestock and poultry feed as eating weed and grass seeds along the roadsides or in pastures.

The bird usually holds its head erect in the dovelike manner, nodding back and forth as it walks. Flight is quick, jerky, and close to the ground. An unusual fluttering sound is made by the wings when the bird flushes. Its call, an often-repeated cooing or two notes on the same pitch with almost equal emphasis, is made almost continuously from dawn to dusk. An occasional *coo-co-hoo* and a *hink-a-doo* call also are made.

The ground dove, slightly smaller than the Inca, weighs little more than an ounce and is about the size of a sparrow. Its chunky body has a short, round tail that often is elevated as the bird walks around on the ground, nodding its head. Whereas the Inca dove is more common in urban areas, the ground dove prefers less-populated rural surroundings. Flight of the ground dove is close to the ground. As

Whitewings get their name from the white bars on their wings.

the bird rises, its wings make a soft, whistling sound, similar to that of the mourning dove, but must less noticeable. Its soft, monotonously repeated call of *woo-oo* seems to merge into a single *wooo* with a rising inflection when heard at a distance. This call, primarily heard during the breeding season, is used to designate territory and courtship.

Another Valley resident is the redbilled pigeon. Similar in size to the domestic pigeon, this bird can be distinguished by its reddish bill. It is a high, swift flier and seeks the tallest timber and brush it can find. Except when standing on sand or gravel bars to drink, the red-billed pigeon seldom is seen on the ground. From February into August the male redbill proclaims its territory with its magnificent jungle voice. It starts with an upwelling *woooooOOOO*, which is quickly followed by three *up-cup-a-coo*'s.

The redbill will fly with whitewings and easily can be misidentified. During the breeding season this pigeon is more likely to be seen singly, in pairs, or in small groups at feeding and watering places. Since the Rio Grande Valley is the redbill's only nesting ground in the United States, its population is restricted to the remaining brush and timber of the area, including some suburban areas. Serious habitat destruction, caused when large native trees are

The mourning dove is the most common and abundant game bird in the United States.

removed or killed, threatens this bird's breeding areas and its continued existence in the Lower Rio Grande Valley.

Unlike the majority of its relatives, which live at low altitudes, the band-tailed pigeon seeks the woodlands of the mountains, breeding between 5,000 and 9,000 feet. It is fairly common in the Guadalupe, Davis, Chinati, and Chisos mountains. If it were not for its preference for mountainous habitat, its tendency to alight in trees, and its yellow feet and legs, the band-tailed pigeon might be mistaken for the slightly smaller rock dove.

This bird is found singly, in pairs, or in small groups during the breeding season, but in fall and winter scattered flocks head for the foothills and open deserts in search of food. The voice of the male has a hollow, owl-like sound. Sitting on a sunny perch atop a dead tree, he hoots his call at irregular intervals in the early morning and late afternoons during the spring and summer.

If these eight species of doves and pigeons are to continue to call Texas home at least part of the year, we must all do our part to make sure their special habitats, especially the native brushlands in the Lower Rio Grande Valley, are protected and perhaps even restored. We cannot allow even one of them to follow the passenger pigeon into extinction.

Mockingbirds

The little gray songster called the mockingbird is a plain-looking bird with thin legs and a slender body that is no more than nine to eleven inches long, including its tail. Both the male and female have gray upper parts and white underparts. Their white wing patches and outer tail feathers show up in flight, and their wings and tails appear rounded. The birds look alike except the female has a little less white in her feathers and is slightly smaller than the male. Since the mockingbird's appearance is less than spectacular, you may wonder why Texas, Tennessee, Florida, Mississippi, and Arkansas have all selected the mocker as their official state bird. The secret of its popularity is its unique singing ability.

Its scientific name, *Mimuspolyglottos,* means "many-tongued mimic," and the Indians called it *Cencontlatolly,* which means "four hundred tongues." Although the Indian name may exaggerate the bird's talents, the mocker not only has a beautiful song of its own, but also can imitate the songs of dozens of other birds. It can warble, whistle, trill, and call, as well as make such interesting sounds as a squeaking gate, croaking frog, barking dog, and chirping cricket. Its mimicry is so good that an electronic device might be needed to tell the original sound from the bird's if it weren't for the mocker's habit of repeating things at least three times.

On one occasion, during an outdoor production of the symphony "Peter and the Wolf," a mockingbird added its own accompaniment to the flutist's portrayal of bird calls in the concert. Needless to say, the audience was delighted

The mockingbird gets its name from its ability to mimic the songs of dozens of other birds, but it also has a beautiful song of its own.

with the bird's mimicry. However, on another occasion, when a mockingbird decided to copy the sound of a traffic policeman's whistle, the bird's efforts were not appreciated. The drivers, who thought all of the whistle sounds were coming from the policeman, were confused about whether to stop or go.

Some people think the mockingbird's song is all mimicry, but researchers tell us that only 10 percent of it falls into this category. The bird actually sings at great lengths in musical phrases that are pure mockingbird song. As the bird sings, it repeats each phrase three to six times, and it can change its tune as often as eighty-seven times in seven minutes. This repetition and the sudden changes of song help distinguish the mockingbird's sounds from those of other birds.

A mockingbird will perch in a tree or sit on a telephone pole or television antenna and sing both day and night. While singing, it spreads its tail, drops or raises its wings, and may even fling itself several feet into the air without missing a note. It has been known to sing for more than an hour without stopping and is especially noisy on moonlit nights. These nighttime concerts often make it unpopular with people who are light sleepers. The mockingbird sings all year long in the southern regions, but it is most vocal throughout its range from February to July and from late August through October. Young mockingbirds can sing, but their songs are described as "soft whisper songs."

The mockingbird lives primarily in the eastern, southern, and midwestern parts of the United States and it can be found throughout Texas. It is adaptable and will make its home in both rural and heavily populated areas. Once a mockingbird stakes out its territory, it will defend that territory against all intruders, including animals much larger than itself. The size or type of opponent does not seem to matter, but the bird is not always successful in driving away the intruder.

Snakes create double trouble for the birds since they feed on both eggs and young. Occasionally a few well-placed pecks will discourage the snake, but all too often the reptile ignores the bird's attack. One observer reported seeing a mockingbird delivering repeated blows to the head and neck of a 2-1/2-foot black snake for more than thirty minutes without causing the snake much injury or making it change direction.

On another, more humorous occasion an observer saw a pig wander over to eat some oranges that had fallen from a tree in which a pair of mockingbirds had built a nest. The birds dived at the pig, pecking it with their beaks and beating it with their wings. But instead of being frightened away by this display of hostility, the pig seemed to enjoy the feel of their beaks pecking on its tough hide. It settled to the ground and rolled over so its broad side would be exposed to their attack. Each peck seemed to increase the pig's enjoyment. After about thirty minutes, the mockingbirds gave up and returned to their nest.

When a photographer recorded a mockingbird's attack on a caracara (a large bird also known as the Mexican eagle), he reported that the mocker's aggressive behavior did not seem to threaten the big bird. However, the nuisance of being dived at and pecked repeatedly did cause the caracara to change its perch a couple of times in an attempt to get rid of the small gray nuisance.

House cats, dogs, and squirrels are easier for the mockers to harass, and on many occasions the birds seem to be teasing the animals. There are numerous accounts of mockers attacking house cats, even though the cats are not near the nest and pose no threat to the birds. Many times the cats cannot even lie in the sunshine and sleep without being dive-bombed by the birds. Another report told how a battling mocker made a pet dog's life miserable. Every time the dog went outside, the bird swooped down and pecked its head and back. Then one day, without any apparent reason, the attacks stopped. The bird either tired of the "game" or accepted the dog as being no threat to its territory.

If you have spent much time watching squirrels playing in the trees, you may have seen one of them being chased by a mockingbird. You probably thought it was funny to see the squirrel leap from limb to limb, race down a tree trunk, run across the ground, and then scoot up another tree with a mockingbird hot on its heels, getting in a jab whenever possible. But if you had been the squirrel, you might not have seen any humor in such persistent attacks.

Squabbles between mockingbirds are not uncommon when territories are being established. Boundary disputes between two birds may be settled with a type of challenge "dance." With heads and tails raised, the birds dart back and forth across the disputed boundary until one gives ground. A mockingbird also may challenge its own image reflected in a window or shiny surface. Males and females establish their own territories except during the breeding season. It is reported that one male and female mocker, which mated with each other for several years in a row, not only established their own separate territories after raising each brood, but also defended these territories against each other. Then when spring arrived,

This mockingbird's attack on a caracara did not seem to threaten the big bird, but it did make the caracara change its perch a couple of times in an attempt to get rid of the small gray nuisance.

the hostilities stopped and the pair got together again in a mutual territory until the next brood was raised.

Young mockers quickly learn to assume the threatening posture, cocking and fanning their tails while uttering sharp notes. These threatening displays are not directed at any particular object at first, but the young soon learn from their parents which animals should receive these threats.

When choosing his mate, the male attracts the female's attention by lifting and spreading his wings high above his back and displaying his white wing patches. He also moves his tail up and down, coos softly, and occasionally runs back and forth in front of her carrying a twig. The two birds may then stand opposite each other and perform a dance pattern, repeating the sequence of steps before flying away.

Both adults are involved in nest building. The male often gathers the materials while the female fits them together to form the nest. Grass, tender roots, and leaves form the lining for the

Mockingbirds 55

small circular nest. It may take the two birds three or four days to build their nest, but the task can be finished in a single day if both birds work at a fast pace. Most nests are found in low bushes, vines, or shrubbery near buildings or along woodland edges on stumps, brush piles, and fence posts. Usually they are three to ten feet off the ground, but they can sometimes be found as low as one foot off the ground or as high as fifty feet.

The three to six eggs, normally laid one a day, are spotted with brown and may vary in color. They can be yellowish or buffy grays or shades of green, blue, brown, or purple. The incubation period is from ten to fourteen days, and the female assumes most of the duties. The male may sit on the eggs if she leaves the nest for a few minutes, but she will probably run him off when she returns. Once the eggs hatch both parents take care of the young. The young stay in the nest for about a week, and then remain close by for another few days or so. The parents will build a new nest if they raise a second brood.

Mockingbirds feed on insects, wild fruit, and weed seeds. During the spring and summer caterpillars, grasshoppers, ants, bees, and other insects make up most of their diet. While feeding on the ground, mockers may spread their wings to expose the white undersides. Some observers believe this "wing-flashing" is used to startle insects such as grasshoppers into moving so they can be seen and caught. During the winter mockingbirds eat mostly vegetable matter. Wild fruits are a favorite whenever they are available, but the birds also may eat or damage some domestic fruits. Because of their insect-eating habits, most people consider them more helpful than harmful, and no one can dispute the fact that the birds truly sing for their supper.

Our small state bird has certainly earned the title "King of Song" and also the reputation for being a scrappy fighter against all odds.

Jays

Colorful, noisy, mischievous, and aggressive are all good words to describe jays, and since they belong to the family that also includes magpies, crows, and ravens, it is not surprising that their most outstanding characteristic is their noisiness. As one unknown poet wrote: "Sometimes your piping is delicious, / And then again it's simply vicious."

Ear-splitting screams may fill the air if an intruder gets too close to the nesting territory, if a roosting owl is located, or even if nothing at all is wrong. Sometimes the jays seem to make noise just for the pleasure of hearing themselves. Henry Thoreau described the sound as being the "unrelenting steel-cold scream of a jay, unmelted, that never flows into a song, a sort of wintry trumpet, screaming cold; hard, tense, frozen music, like the winter sky itself." Although jays have an apparently endless supply of whistles and calls of their own, they can also mimic the sounds of other birds, especially the red-shouldered, red-tailed, and sparrow hawks.

With its stout, sharp-pointed, all-purpose bill, the jay can hammer, crack, crush, probe, split, and tear its food. No nut is too hard to crack. If the jay encounters difficulty in holding and cracking a particularly tough nut, it is not unusual for the bird to wedge the nut in a log in order to give a more effective blow with its beak. It will eat almost anything, including mice, insects, and carrion, but most of its diet consists of nuts and seeds. When an abundance of food is available, the bird buries its surplus nuts, then digs them up again when food is scarce. Jays have a rather tarnished reputation because they occasionally raid other bird's nests and eat the eggs and young, but the jay is not known to endanger any other bird species by this practice.

Now that you know a little about jays in general, let's take a closer look at each of the five species that are found in Texas, starting with the blue jay. Its bright blue color, black and white markings, and head crest make this bird easy to identify, and it is one of the most striking species found in the yards, gardens, and parks of East and Central Texas. Although it originally was a bird of the woods, preferring pine, oak, mixed hardwoods, and their edges, it has adapted well to humans and the urban habitat. In wilder areas it can be found in streamside woodlands, prairie tree groves, and wooded hillsides. Predicting its behavior in different situations would be difficult; it may silently follow a person through the woods in an almost curious manner or accompany the same person with loud, raucous cries that alert every animal within hearing distance that there is an intruder in the woods.

In autumn, when most other birds are quiet, the blue jay usually displays its vocal talents. The sounds may be a bell-like *tul-ull* call, a soft conversational-type chatter between jays, or harsh hawklike screams. From concealment, the blue jay also may deliver a whisperlike song with barely audible, sweep lisping notes resembling those of such small birds as the chickadee. When nesting season arrives the blue jay becomes almost silent and furtive. During the courtship ceremony the male feeds his mate while they exchange low whistles. Then the pair collect twigs which they haul around until a suitable nest site is found. Both birds help build the platform of twigs, bark, grass, and paper. They also have been known to appropriate another bird's nest and remodel it to suit themselves. The four to six olive- or buff-colored eggs, marked with brown spots, hatch in about seventeen days. While the female is incubating the eggs,

Its habit of letting its tail hang down while perched in repose is a good field identification mark for the scrub jay.

the male hops silently up the tree, as if following an invisible spiral staircase, to bring her food. Later he also will bring food to the young. The pair will defend their nest from all intruders, including humans.

Three-fourths of the blue jay's diet consists of vegetable matter, and the jay stores acorns and other nuts for winter use by burying them in the ground. Some of these buried seeds grow to trees when the jays forget to retrieve them. The animal portion of its menu includes spiders, snails, salamanders, tree frogs, mice, and insects. It is among the few birds that eat hairy caterpillars, and it will even rip open cocoons to get to the pupae inside.

The flight of the blue jay is steady and direct, but not particularly swift. It moves easily through the trees with full, regular, quick flaps of its wings. Except during its erratic migrations or wanderings in October, the bird seldom flies across open country. Blue jays make a habit of sunning themselves. As the bird sits with its breast facing the sun, it raises its wings to expose the under plumage to the warm rays. It also lies breast down on the ground with its wings spread to warm its back and rump.

Blue jays also engage in an activity known as anting, in which they gather a beakful of ants and excitedly rub them over their feathers. Naturalists have watched as many as 150 different species of birds anting, but have failed to come up with any clear-cut explanations for the activity. Some have suggested that the formic acid secreted by the ants may deter lice and mites from the feathers. Others seem to think that the birds just like the feeling of the ant secretion on their bodies since they react with ecstasy to the experience, as a cat does to catnip.

Another activity they seem to enjoy is harassing predatory birds such as herons, owls, hawks, or crows. A flock of noisy jays will surround the bird, screaming and darting at it with bluff and bluster. Owls seem to trigger the jay's harassing response most often. Occasionally, the jays will tease one of these predatory birds by imitating the cry of a wounded bird, but the joke can backfire. If not all of the mischievous jays escape in time, one of them may become a meal for the predator.

Another member of the jay family, the crestless Mexican jay, is found in the foothill country along the Mexican border. It prefers the juniper-pine-oak woods of the Chisos Mountains and is common in the Big Bend National Park. Mexican jays band together in small groups and nest in loose colonies. Several members of the flock may pitch in to help a nesting pair build a platform nest of green twigs. Four or five plain green or spotted green eggs are laid by the female in May. The whole colony will help feed and guard the hatchlings. Within a month the young are able to accompany the flock as they forage for food.

The birds feed on cicadas, grasshoppers, other insects, acorns, nuts, seeds, wild fruits, and occasionally the eggs or young of small birds. In the Chisos Mountains they frequently eat the flowering parts of century plants and drink the nectar and other plant juices from the agave blossoms. Flight of the Mexican jay is strong, darting, and seldom sustained. To take advantage of the protection the trees offer, they move through them rather than fly over them.

The green jay is the tropical member of the jay family, and it also has no head crest. Found in the United States only in South Texas, its green, yellow, and blue plumage makes it the gem of the woodlands. Mexicans call it *Pajaro verde*, green bird. It is most numerous in willow trees and tall brush along the lower Rio Grande and its tributaries, but also can be found during the summer in mesquite woodlands some distance from water. In those areas where native evergreens have been cleared, flocks of green jays flit through citrus groves during the cooler months. In small flocks, they chase each other through the trees. Any human invasion quickly brings them out of the dense cover to investigate. They may scream at the person for a while before disappearing silently into the brush. The green jay is skillful at staying concealed when stalked, but often ironically gives itself away once the hunt is over. When the stalker turns to leave, several of the jays may scream at it and some may even come to the edge of the brush to look the intruder over.

In the spring the noisy flocks disband, and pairs locate thickets in which to breed. Like most of their relatives, green jays are quiet near their nests. On a platform of rootlets and twigs the female lays three to five brown-spotted eggs. The base color of the eggs may be gray, greenish, or buff. Like the other members of the family, green jays eat both animal and vegetable matter, and large insects are a favorite source of protein. Picnic tables and garbage cans installed along U.S. Highway 77 have become an attraction for feeding birds. They often can be seen waiting in the nearby evergreen oaks for the picnickers to leave so they can fly out and pick up any bits of hamburger, french fries, or other foods left behind. The green jay is indeed one of the most beautiful garbage collectors in the area.

The Steller's jay is the dark member of the family, with its black and blue plumage and long black crest. It makes its home in Texas in the western yellow

The Steller's jay, the only crested jay in the western United States, feeds on insects, acorns, nuts, pine seeds, wild fruits, and an occasional egg.

pine and Douglas fir high in the Guadalupe Mountains. During the cooler months family groups wander down to the foothills and valleys to scout out camping areas and other human locations where they can pick up table scraps and edible trash. The Steller's jay also may raid the storehouse trees and telephone poles of the acorn woodpecker. Bounding from branch to branch, frequently moving up successive limbs in a tree in a sort of spiral, the Steller's jay feeds on insects, acorns, nuts, pine seeds, wild fruits, and an occasional egg. The bird may flick its wings and tail and whack its bill on a branch while foraging. This action probably causes insects to reveal themselves to the hungry bird.

When the breeding season rolls around, the Steller's jay builds a foundation of twigs and adds a deep cup of grass or moss. It then plasters the structure with mud and lines it with pine needles or rootlets. Into it the female lays three to five greenish white eggs specked with brown and lavender.

The final member of the jay family found in Texas is the crestless scrub jay. This shy and elusive bird is seen most often as a blue-gray streak flashing through the brush. In the Trans-Pecos hills and canyons it can be found in piñon, juniper, and oak scrub, but on the Edwards Plateau it lives in thickets of oak and junipers. Individual birds occasionally winter along willow-lined streams in the Panhandle canyons.

A typical and often observed action of the scrub jay is its swift, graceful dive from a high vantage point into a thicket. It frequently uses bushtop lookout perches, and when it descends to the ground, it feeds on insects, acorns, piñon nuts, wild fruits, and berries. It also raids the nests of small birds for eggs and young. Feeding flocks often converse in odd chuckles, as do their blue jay cousins; however, they are not as boisterous. A frequently heard sound in the Edwards Plateau is a scrub jay vocalization that sounds like the sudden ripping of a piece of canvas. Occasionally the bird also delivers the low throat rattle common to all Texas jays. A soft whispery, cooing song is made by the well-hidden scrub jay in the spring.

During the 1940s and 1950s ranchers in the central and western parts of the Edwards Plateau cleared most of the cedar from their land. Since the scrub jay prefers a habitat of scrubby juniper or cedar and oak, this brush clearing forced the bird to move its range eastward about a hundred miles to the cedar brakes west of Austin. Before 1950 the scrub jay had been unknown in the Austin area.

Jays may not be one of your favorite birds, but even with all of their faults, these colorful loudmouths add beauty and liveliness wherever they are found.

Hummingbirds

Tiniest of all the birds, the hummingbird is an amazing creature — probably the most unusual member of the bird family. Of all of the billions of hummingbirds that may have lived throughout the ages, no fossils have been found that would give clues to this bird's ancestry. They live only in the western hemisphere, and most of them are found in Central and South America, although they range from Alaska to the tip of Argentina. Although there are more than 300 species, only 18 are found regularly in the United States. Of these, 9 are common to Texas, and an additional 6 have made accidental appearances in the state.

Perhaps the most amazing thing about the tiny hummingbird is its energy level. From a standing start, it can rev up its speed to an unbelievable sixty miles per hour in a distance of three feet. It has the highest energy output per unit of body weight of any animal in the world. According to the Institute of Aeronautical Sciences, a hovering hummingbird consumes about 726 Btu of energy per pound per hour. This is very close to the 750 Btu consumed by a helicopter in flight.

Comparisons with human energy use are even more astounding. When hovering, the hummingbird's energy output is ten times that of a man running at nine miles per hour (the highest output of human energy known, and a speed that cannot be maintained for more than half an hour). The average man burns about 3,500 calories a day. If the daily output of a hummingbird were calculated for a 170-pound man, he would need to burn about 155,000 calories. Translated into food intake, to keep up with the energy a hummingbird burns each day, a human would have to eat 285 pounds of hamburger or 370 pounds of potatoes.

Keeping its miniature power plant

Light and motion are required for the hummer's throat feathers to flash their vivid colors. This black-chinned hummingbird's throat flashes a beautiful royal purple stripe.

fueled requires the hummingbird to feed every ten to fifteen minutes. However, since the bird cannot maintain such a demanding feeding program on a twenty-four-hour basis, it deals with the problem by going into a hibernationlike state at night. While in this condition, known as torpor, it is unable to move. Its body temperature drops to that of the surrounding air and its energy rate drops to one-twentieth of the

food. The bill is long and sharp and can plunge deep into the flowers or slash them open to get at the nectar. The tongue, which is extremely long, can be extended beyond the bill. (Hummingbirds and woodpeckers are the only birds that can do this.) The front part of the tongue is split, and the outer edges curl for part of the length to form two parallel tubes that are used like straws to suck nectar from the flowers. The outer edges are frayed like a brush to make it easier for the bird to gather insects.

Because of its high energy output and its dependence on plant nectar, the hummingbird's northward migration is timed closely to the blooming of certain flowers that will meet its feeding needs. Pollen, which may be transferred to the bird's head as it dips deep into the blossom, is spread to other flowers as the bird continues its feeding. This makes the hummer one of the important pollinators of tubular flowers.

Its flight is another characterictic that makes the hummingbird unique, and it is the reason the bird needs so much energy. It cannot soar the way other birds do, or just flap its wings a few times and glide. Its wings must be in constant motion to keep it in the air. A few other species, such as the ospreys, kingfishers, and sunbirds, can hover somewhat in flight, but only the hummingbirds can hold their bodies still in mid-air with their fast-beating wings. No other bird can match the flying skill of the hummingbird, which not only hovers, but also flies up, down, and backwards.

Since its wings must be used for long periods of time without rest, and since these wings move extremely fast, the hummingbird's breast muscles are huge in proportion to its size. They weigh about a third of its total weight, and

When a Mexican green violet-ear hummingbird paid a rare visit across the border to Texas, birders came from all over the country to watch it sip from a backyard feeder in Austin and to record the event on film.

daytime level. Even at this lower level, the energy used by the bird is about the same as that of a human exercising vigorously. Although most animals cannot be awakened from torpor quickly, the hummingbird's arousal is almost instantaneous.

Sugar is the main energy source for the hummingbird, usually in the form of nectar from tubular-shaped flowers.

The bird also gets protein by eating small spiders, which are plucked from their webs, and insects, which are caught on the wing. The birds often are seen feeding amidst swarms of small insects or catching those attracted to oozing tree sap. It is estimated that about 25 percent of their diet is insects.

The hummingbird's tongue and bill are perfectly adapted for obtaining its the muscles used to draw the wings upward are almost as powerful as those that drive the wings down. In relation to its body size, the hummer also has the largest heart in the bird world. A large, strong heart is needed to circulate the oxygen and nutrients needed for this bird's high-energy life-style.

The hummingbird's narrow wings have no more than a four-inch span, and those of some species are even smaller. The "hand" portion of its wing is the longest part; the "arm" portion is quite short. The joints at the "wrist" and "elbow" are fused to give the wings a strong frame, and they are attached to the shoulders in such a way as to allow movement in any direction. The wings beat in a figure-eight pattern at such tremendous speeds that they almost vanish in a blur. This wing movement produces the humming sound that gives the birds their name. The power of flight in most birds is in the downstroke. The upstroke is merely a recovery motion to prepare the bird for another powerful downstroke. However, in the all-directional flight of the hummingbird both strokes are powerful. Forward flight is generated on the downstroke. When the tiny bird reaches speeds of up to sixty miles per hour, its wings may be beating as fast as eighty times a second, depending on the species. Some may beat at an even faster rate.

To hover, the hummingbird tilts its body and wings into a more vertical position. This causes the main flight feathers to push air downward instead of backward. The downstroke and upstroke provide lift but not forward movement. On the downstroke, the wings are tilted so that they force air downwards and the bird upwards. At the end of the downstroke, the wings twist 90 degrees. This forces air downward on the upstroke as well. To fly backward the wings are tilted slightly so that air also is forced forward, which drives the hummingbird back. Hummingbirds do not take off by leaping into the air as other birds do. Instead, they lift off with rapid wingbeats. Specialized filming has shown that a hummingbird taking off from a thin twig actually pulls the twig up a little before letting go as it rises. Its short, thin legs and tiny feet are not used for walking or hopping. The bird depends almost entirely on its wings to move from place to place, using its feet and legs only for perching or sidling along a tree limb.

The courtship flight of the male hummingbird is a stunning display of aerial acrobatics that varies according to the species. No other bird can equal his speed and agility. Like a stunt flyer, he may start his performance with a power dive in a U-shaped curve before the watching female. Once he has her attention, he really puts on a show. For variation, he may dart at the female like a bullet, brake quickly, shoot straight up for fifty feet, and then plummet back, catching himself in mid-air just beside or in front of her. Every movement reflects the dazzling colors of his iridescent neck feathers and attempts to convince her that he would make a fine mate.

These beautiful iridescent colors are a trademark of the hummer, especially the male's flashing, jewellike throat patches, known as gorgets. These colors often are used to name the species. For example there are the ruby-throated hummingbird common in the eastern portion of the state and a rare blue-throated hummingbird in the southwestern part of the state. The most abundant hummer, which lives in the central and western parts of the state, is the black-chinned hummingbird, but when its black throat feathers catch the light they flash to a beautiful royal purple stripe. The brilliant colors displayed by the hummingbirds are not caused by pigments in the feathers. Instead, these colors are structural, which means they are produced by reflected or refracted light. The feathers are a mosaic of tiny clear platelets, each filled with air bubbles. Like prisms, they produce the colors we see. In order for the vivid colors to reflect, the bird must be in a direct light coming from behind the observer. When the bird is in motion, the shimmering colors are in constant change, and sometimes even disappear.

In the early days of our history, before birds were protected by laws, the hummer's beautiful feathers were so attractive to humans that people used the birds in large numbers for decorations and clothing. When the Spaniards were exploring the New World, they found Aztecs at Montezuma's court wearing cloaks made entirely of hummingbird skins. Records also show that at the time the Pilgrims were settling New England, they occasionally saw Indians wearing a hummingbird in one ear like an earring. And in Victorian times the birds were killed so their feathers could be used to make artificial flowers and hat decorations. If such use had not been made illegal, hummingbirds might have been eliminated and we would not have an opportunity to watch the males perform their aerial acrobatics and flash their beautiful feathers.

The courtship flights of the males may go on for as long as a month before mating occurs. However, once his performance has produced the desired results and breeding is accomplished, the male hummingbird is quickly on his way. The female must handle the nest-building duties and raise the young on her own. Using plant down, fibers, and spiderwebs, she builds a small cuplike

A backyard feeder will allow you to attract hummingbirds, such as these rubythroats, but proper care and maintenance of the feeder is a necessity.

nest about the size of a half-dollar. The spider webs help hold it together and are used to anchor it to a branch. The outside is covered with moss, lichens, or other materials plucked from the tree branch to camouflage it and make it look like part of the branch. Into the tiny cup she lays two pea-sized white eggs that hatch in a couple of weeks. The young are born blind, naked, and completely dependent on the mother bird. She must now feed her hungry offspring as well as herself.

The feeding process can be startling the first time it is observed. The female braces her tail against the side of the nest and plunges her daggerlike bill down the young one's throat to the hilt. She then starts a jabbing action that looks as if she is stabbing it. What she actually is doing is pumping the young bird full of regurgitated, semi-digested remains of insects and nectar. The amount of time the young spend in the nest varies with the species, but the average is about twenty days. Before taking off on its first flight, the young hummer sits on the edge of the nest and tries its wings. It begins moving them slowly, building up to a fast buzz, holding on to the edge to keep from actually taking off. After practicing several times, the young bird masters the art of balancing and rising and is ready to fly.

Hummingbirds have few predators since their quickness and agility in flight usually prevent other birds and mammals from catching them. However, it has been reported that occasionally a large frog or fish may catch one as the hummer flies low over the water, and spider webs or thistles sometimes snare them. Collisions with picture windows and glass also can be fatal, but the greatest hazards they face are the weather and a shortage of food that might occur when a late frost kills the flowers they feed on.

Migration is quite a challenge for the hummingbird, especially for the ruby-throats, which may travel 2,500 miles from Alaska to Mexico and fly nonstop across the Gulf of Mexico. Since the bird cannot feed during its 500-mile trip over the water, it must store a tremendous amount of fat (five times as much as normal) all over its body to sustain it during the flight. Many migrating hummers concentrate in the coastal area of Texas for a few weeks before heading for their winter homes in Mexico and Central America. Coastal residents take full advantage of the layover to enjoy these beautiful birds.

Flowering plants that attract hummingbirds include the Turk's cap, morning-glory, silver-leaf sunflower, coral vine, esperanza or yellow alder, trumpet vine, all honeysuckles, coral-bean, and hibiscus. Some others with appetizing nectar are the azalea, bee balm, bergamot, columbine, tiger lily, larkspur, nasturtium, scarlet sage, beauty bush, butterfly bush, weigela, cardinal flower, coral bells, foxglove, snapdragon, scarlet salvia, pea tree, mimosa tree, and horse chestnut.

Watching hummingbirds in your own back yard is an activity that provides hours of entertainment, and the birds are easy to attract to commercial hummingbird feeders. Most of these feeders feature artificial red flowers because the birds seem to be attracted to this color. Such a backyard feeder will permit you to watch these fantastic fliers, but proper care and maintenance are necessary if you do not want to harm them.

There is some controversy as to the best type of sweet liquid to use in these feeders. Some people believe it should be a honey-water mixture because of its added nutrients. However, a honey mixture ferments quickly, especially in the heat of summer, and the fungus that results is harmful to the birds. It causes the bird's tongue to swell and prevents it from feeding. And as we learned earlier, if a hummer cannot eat frequently, it will not survive. If honey is used, the mixture of one part honey to five parts water should be boiled briefly to sterilize it and then allowed to cool before you place it in the feeder. The feeder also should be cleaned and sterilized between each honey-water filling to help prevent the growth of fungus. This may have to be done every few hours when the weather is hot.

The easiest liquid to use in hummingbird feeders is a sugar-water mixture that is one part sugar to four or five parts water. Most birders recommend that it not be mixed stronger because too much sugar may cause liver problems for the birds, and the natural nectar they get from flowers is usually no more than 20 to 25 percent sugar. If it is not sipped away by the hummers, this sugar water also will need to be changed every few days to keep it from fermenting, and the feeder scrubbed at each filling to prevent molds from growing.

When you attract hummingbirds to a feeder, be prepared to see them fighting and squabbling among themselves over the feeders or territory. Occasionally one male will decided the feeder belongs to him and he will dive-bomb or try to chase away any other hummer that might try to sip at the same feeder. But no matter how bad-tempered they may appear to be with each other, we can still appreciate the unique characteristics that make them such a delightful member of the bird world.

Illustration Credits

Index

Introducing Birds to Young Naturalists was composed into type on a Compugraphic digital phototypesetter in ten point Palatino with two points of spacing between the lines. Palatino was also selected for display. The book was designed by Jim Billingsley, typeset by Metricomp, Inc., printed offset by Hart Graphics, Inc., and bound by Custom Bookbinders, Inc. The paper on which the book is printed is designed for an effective life of at least three hundred years.

Texas A&M University Press
College Station